Why Can't Mondays Be More Like Sundays?

Dr. Paul Cannings

Lighting Source, Inc. | *La Vergne Tennessee*

Copyright C 2008, by Paul Cannings, D. Phil

Why Can't Mondays Be More Like Sundays?
ISBN 978-0-615-22292-9

Please send your comments and requests for information to the address below:

Power Walk Ministries
7350 West T.C. Jester Blvd.
Houston, TX 77088
Telephone (281) 260-7402
www.lwfellowshipchurch.org

All Rights Reserved. No part of this publication may be reproduced, stored in a retrieval system, or transmitted in any form or by any means –electronically, mechanically, photocopy, recording, or any other—except for brief quotations in printed reviews, without the prior permission of the author or Power Walk Ministries.

Printed in the United States of America.

Scripture quotations are from the New American Standard Bible (NASB), unless otherwise noted.

For more information concerning other products we offer including:

"Biblical Answers For the 21st Century Church" ISBN 978-0-9779840-3-6
"Vision to Ministry" ISBN 978-0-9779840-2-8
"Jesus and Money" ISBN 978-0-9779840-4-6
"Keeping Love Alive Series" for strengthening marriages or the
"Leadership Training Series" for training leaders

Visit our website at **www.lwfellowshipchurch.org/**

For more information about speaking engagements please contact us by telephone at (281) 260-7402.

Contents

Preface .... *i*

Acknowledgements .... *iii*

1. *When Temptations Strike* *4*

    Understanding Temptations 6

    How Faith Helps Us Overcome Temptations 11

2. *Living through Adversity* *19*

    Jesus and Suffering 21

    God Cares—Do you? 21

    My Personal Story 23

    Believe in Your Heart 23

    Abide in Him 25

    Hold on to His Word 26

    Serve Him Faithfully 27

    Faithfulness Produces Trust 30

    Maintain Your Integrity—Do not Violate God's Trust 30

    Faithfulness in Adversity leads to Blessings 33

    Remain Faithful Despite Your Blessings 34

3. *Dealing with Hopelessness* *37*

    Struggling with Hopelessness 38

    Jesus Meets You at Your Point of Need 39

    Come to Jesus 41

    Jesus Identifies with Your Struggles.................... 45

    Jesus Is Able To Solve Problems 46

4. *Guilty, but not Condemned* *49*

    Understanding Accusations 50

    When We Sin 53

    Christ is Your Advocate....................................... 56

    When Others Sin 57

    When You Stand Accused 59

    In Conclusion 62

5. *Loving the Unlovable* *64*

    A Deeper Understanding...................................... 65

    Commit to Obey Christ 68

    Role of the Tongue 70

    Operating like Jesus 70

    Vengeance Belongs to the Lord 71

    Love in Action 72

    Praying for Your Enemy 73

    A Believer's Role... 75

    When you Love the Unlovable 79

6. *A Better Sacrifice* *83*

    Belief or Faith? 83

    A Worthy Offering... 87

    Dependency and Worship 91

    A Greater Dependency... 93

	Offering for Recognition	94
	God the Supplier	95
7.	*Don't Give Up*	*98*
	Faith That Does Not Quit	99
	The Result of Faith	108
8.	*Faith that Blesses*	*115*
	Faith will Lead You to Jesus	116
	Faith will Lead You to Obey	118
	Faith will Lead You to Bless!	120
	Faith will Lead You to Wait to be Blessed	124
9.	*Faith that Rocks*	*127*
	Life's Comfort or God's Direction	128
	Choosing to Endure	132
	Understanding Reward from the Father	135
	Fear and Punishment!	138
	Growing Up	141
	The Legacy	141
	Faith that Rocks!	145
10.	*Living Life with a Punch*	*151*
	Everlasting Peace	152
	Wisdom from God	156
	Living His Name	160
About Power Walk Ministries		*165*

Preface

Faith has become a misery to uncover rather than a joy to experience. This book seeks to explain how faith can become an intricate part of a believer's life causing a believers relationship with God to be intimate, meaningful and productive.

Faith is not something a person has as a result of positive thinking. A person can be very positive, but still struggle and eventually become frustrated and confused. Positive thinking is effective, but it must function within the scope of God's Word. Positive thinking in itself is not faith.

Some people believe that if they speak something into being and believe it with all their heart, God will bring it to pass. They believe that this is a strong sign of faith. Many people have done this and experience a lot of debt. Faith is not speaking something into being, because then God would need to have faith when He spoke the world into existence. God did not need faith; God exercised His power.

Some people view the people in the Bible who walked powerfully are of something special, but not normal. Some may not say this, but they look at these great acts of God as special to those like Abraham, Isaac and Jacob. It is almost as if God exercised His power less and less over time. God is still as powerful. The issue is not God. It is understanding, within a Biblical context, what is true faith.

Preface ii

    This book seeks to make faith something that is real, powerful and pleasing to God. It is not just for a believer's spiritual growth; but also for an intimate experience of God daily. God is experienced as real in a believer's life. Powerfully functioning and thus providing the believer a sense of peace, they experience God at work in and through their lives daily.

Acknowledgements

I would like to thank by wife, Everette, of 28 years, and children, Paul Jr. and Pierre, for their continued support and encouragement. My family and I have taken many `steps of faith' over the years and God has truly demonstrated His faithfulness to us. They have been, and continue to be, the love of my life and I thank God for them and the relationship He has established among us through the years.

I would like to thank the Power Walk Ministry volunteers for their labor of love and commitment to the ongoing development of the ministry. Power Walk Ministry has benefited tremendously from their consistent efforts to enhance the vision of the ministry. Without them, the process of developing this book would have been very difficult.

There are many people who have made a lot of sacrifices in order to make this book possible. To them all, I say thank you very much.

CHAPTER 1

When Temptations Strike

And Jesus full of the Holy Spirit, returned from the Jordan and was led about by the Spirit in the wilderness for forty days, being tempted by the devil. And He ate nothing during those days, and when they had ended, He became hungry. (Luke 4:1-2)

We are all tempted and often yield to temptation. No matter how hard we try, we fail time and time again. Why is that? Much of our failure is because we don't use our strongest weapon, the Holy Spirit. The Holy Spirit is literally God living in us. He loves us and wants us to be holy. And when we trust Him, walk by faith, and live in consistent obedience to His Word, He strengthens us and helps us to resist temptation. This chapter helps us to understand that we can fight temptation with His help.

A teenager's father was heading out on a business trip with his wife. He told his son, "I'm going. Make sure that you clearly understand that you must not drive my car."

Then the father sat the son down, looked him in the eye, and said, "I don't want you to drive my car, not even for a second. I don't want you to start it; I don't want you to take it outside the garage to wash it. I don't want you to take the vacuum cleaner inside the car to vacuum it. I don't want you to turn on the radio in the car. I want you to leave my car alone." Finally, he took the keys and put them on the kitchen counter. Then he went on his business trip for several days.

Upon his return, the son came to the father and said, "Dad, here are your keys."

The father said, "Son, I left the keys on the kitchen counter. Why do you have my keys?"

The son replied, "Dad, I've been carrying these keys around trying not to drive your car. Why did you leave your keys behind?"

The father explained, "Son, you would have never learned to resist temptation if I had not left the car keys behind. I left the keys behind because I wanted you to learn not to respond to temptation."

The Gospel of Luke tells us that the Holy Spirit led Jesus to the wilderness (Luke 4:1). The Holy Spirit led "Human God" to the wilderness--not Christ, *deity*, but Human God, *Jesus*. When Jesus was tempted, He could experience as a human being all the pressures that we experience when we are tempted. He could feel all of the concerns that we feel as human beings when tempted. Please do not miss the key issue. Luke wants us to know that Jesus was "full of the Holy Spirit" (Luke 4:1) as He was led to the wilderness.

In Luke 4:14, he says, "And Jesus returned to Galilee in the power of the Spirit." Now stop right here and read the above lines again. We have to understand that between being led to and overcoming the temptation, Christ never loses the fullness of the Holy Spirit.

Do you know that many years ago when the military first put a submarine under water, the submarine's walls would break and burst into many pieces? They soon learned that a submarine required equal pressure on the inside in order to match the pressure on the outside in the depths of the sea, or it would burst. The pressure on our inside must be present in order to resist the forces on the outside or we will crumble and fall apart like a submarine in the deep sea.

Listen, God never takes away our ability to get a credit card and walk through the mall and see the wonderful dresses and suits in those glass cases. God never takes away the lottery tickets when we go to the store. God never creates a utopia for us so that we may live righteously. However, God does offer us His Spirit on the inside so we can deal with the temptations on the outside. He knows that if the pressure on the inside matches the pressure on the outside, we will be able to resist temptation.

Understanding Temptations

Temptations come and will continue coming as long as we are alive. The world offers endless temptations that come with the promise that life will be better once one succumbs to temptation. Temptation may come in the form of a woman at the office smiling at you every day. There may be that guy whispering sweet nothings to you when you and your husband are not getting along. He says all the things your husband is not saying and he says it every day. It could also be that candy aisle at the grocery store while you're dieting. It could even be a beautiful Jaguar idling next to your car at the traffic light, while your car is shaking and smoking.

Well, all of us fail miserably many times when it comes to temptations. That's why many of us are in debt. We are living above our means. Why? Temptation! We just cannot resist. That's why many of us are stressed out, because we bought a car we cannot afford. Temptation! As a matter of fact, I spoke at a revival once and after the revival they had dinner and I was sitting next to a guy who sold Cadillacs.

I wondered why he sat next to a preacher, so I asked him, "How do you get people to buy $50,000, $60,000, $70,000 vehicles? After all, the car still does not have a restroom! You still have to change the tires the same way; turn the steering wheel the same way; turn on the radio the same way' sit on that seat the same way; and do the same stuff you do in a $15,000 vehicle or a $5,000 vehicle? How do you get somebody to spend 70,000 dollars?"

He said, "I work with people's senses. I make a person get in the car; hear it; touch it; and then drive it. And that person will write me a check."

Interesting, right?

It is not just the world system that is organized against God to tempt us. There's another reason why we get tempted, even though we may be living a righteous life. The devil accuses us before our God, day and night (Revelation 12:10).

Remember Job? What was Job actually doing wrong? Nothing! But Satan went up and questioned the Lord: "Does Job fear God for nothing? Have You not made a hedge about him and his house and all that he has, on every side? You have blessed the work of his hands, and his possessions have increased in the land. But put forth Your hand now and touch all that he has; he will surely curse You to Your face" (Job 1:9-11). If you are familiar with the book of Job you know that Satan did everything possible to tempt Job to turn away from God.

Well, Satan *is* the devil, but there are times when Satan doesn't have to go to God. It is because we give him a foothold in our lives.

Ephesians 4:26-27 says, "Be angry, and yet do not sin; do not let the sun go down on your anger, and do not give the devil an opportunity."

Wrong thoughts lead to malice, wickedness, slander, envy and other sins. The devil does not need to go to heaven. Why? Because time and time again we break the hedge of protection that God has put around us (Hebrews 1:14) and let in the evil forces.

James 1:13-15 declares that God does not tempt us. We are tempted when we do what David did. David looked--and looked again. Because he kept looking, his flesh desired Bathsheba. Sin was conceived and it brought forth death. Yes, this was the same David who could go before Goliath with five smooth stones and use one to kill him and the same David who killed the lion and the bear. Did Satan need to go to heaven to pull him down? No! David allowed sin to conceive and as a result gave Satan a foothold into his life.

The Lord's Prayer contains this line: "And do not lead us into temptation, but deliver us from evil" (Matthew 6:13). If you refer to the temptations of

Jesus: who led Jesus to Satan? The Holy Spirit! (Matthew 4:1)

Even though God does not tempt us, there are times when God does not remove temptations from our lives. So the question is why would Christ permit us to face temptations? "Because greater is He who is in you than he who is in the world" (1 John 4:4).

Why do coaches take their teams to football games? They know that if their team follows their instructions, they have the potential to win. As each opponent comes and goes, the team grows. The stronger the team, the greater is their potential to beat better opponents.

Therefore, it must not surprise us that there are times when Christ leaves the keys on the kitchen counter. Because we live in a world that offers countless evil possibilities, we must daily learn to overcome the attacks of the enemy. The more we rely on the power of God to meet temptations, the better the pressure on the inside will be, and the better we can adjust to the ever-changing pressure on the outside.

Before we move further, understand that a test is not a sin. A temptation is not a sin. Satan tempted, or tested, Jesus in order to destroy Jesus, the Son of God. A test is a solicitation to sin. The Holy Spirit took Jesus to the wilderness and proved that Jesus is the King of kings. Jesus relied totally on the powerful Word of God and trusted in it when He was solicited to sin. When Christ leads us to a test, you must understand what God is doing with the test. When we are obedient to His Word during the test, Christ reveals our ability to overcome the test with the help of the Holy Spirit.

"You are from God, little children, and have overcome them; because greater is He who is in you than he who is in the world." (1 John 4:4-5)

"But the Helper, the Holy Spirit, whom the Father will send in My name, He will teach you all things, and bring to your remembrance all that I said to you. Peace I leave with you; My peace I give to you; not as the world gives do I give to you. Do not let your heart be troubled, nor let it be fearful." (John 14:26-27)

When we say no to that man; no to that woman; when we say no to that lottery ticket; when we decide to discipline ourselves and be patient, God says, "You're growing, son! You are doing great, my daughter! Well done!" The pressure on the inside, as in the case of a submarine, powerfully matches the pressure on the outside.

"How blessed is the man who does not walk in the counsel of the wicked, nor stand in the path of the sinners, nor sit in the seat of scoffers! But his delight is in the law of the Lord, and in His law he meditates day and night. He will be like a tree firmly planted by streams of water, which yields its fruit in due season and its leaf does not wither; and in whatever he does, he prospers." (Psalm 1:1-3)

To experience the inner working of the Holy Spirit is to decide to obey the Word of God rather than respond to influences of the flesh.

"For those who are according to the flesh set their minds on the things of the flesh, but those who are according to the Spirit, the things of the Spirit. For the mind set on the flesh is death, but the mind set on the Spirit is life and peace, because the mind set on the flesh is hostile toward God; for it does not subject itself to the law of God, for it is not even able to do so, and those who are in the flesh cannot please God." (Romans 8:5-8)

It is the commitment to obey God's Word (just like Christ held onto God's Word in the midst of temptation) that nurtures the indwelling of the Spirit of God in our lives (1 John 2:3-6). Each test coupled with obedience increases the powerful influence of the Holy Spirit. It is in a test we are more compelled to obey God, trust Him, and to grow in Him.

How Faith Helps Us Overcome Temptations

Focus on the Master. I used to coach a group of basketball players. I remember during a basketball game the other team kept scoring and our guys just kept backing off and it was difficult. So I called a time out and said, "Guys, we got a major problem. You keep playing their game. You can't beat them at their game, because we don't play their game. We must play our game."

Our team stopped playing the game the other team wanted us to play and we won the game! As you attempt to overcome the temptations in your life, you must focus on the One who is willing to help you through your temptations. If you focus on the temptation, you'll lose. If you focus on your Savior, you will win.

A man wanted to train his dog to eat only what he wanted the dog to eat. So the man put a big piece of bloody meat right in front of the dog, right when the dog was hungry, and said, "No!" Initially, the dog could not bear the temptation and gobbled down the meat. The man kept repeating the test over and over again until the dog finally learned never to look at the meat. The dog trusted that his master would never leave him hungry and learned to keep looking at his master and wait on his instructions.

Our problem is that in the midst of temptation, when the forces are great, we do not let the inside dominate the outside. Instead of focusing on our Master, we prefer to look at the temptation and surrender to the temptation.

"Therefore, since we have so great a cloud of witnesses surrounding us, let us also lay aside every encumbrance and the sin which so easily entangles us, and let us run with endurance the race that is set before us, fixing our eyes on Jesus, the author and perfecter of faith, who for the joy set before Him endured the cross, despising the shame, and has sat down at the right hand of the throne of God." (Hebrews 12:1-2)

Quit complaining. Whatever you may be going through, quit complaining about the test, because the test is not a sin. We want this utopia in our lives and we get mad at God for the temptations. "God, give me a utopia. When I get up, let the car start by itself. God, don't let me feel sleepy. Let me feel energized, ready to work hard and excited about a new day. Don't let me feel bad. Take away my troubles. Help me to have a great day." We want utopia, but God wants us to quit complaining.

"Do all things without grumbling or disputing; so that you will prove yourselves to be blameless and innocent, children of God above reproach in the midst of a crooked and perverse generation, among whom you appear as lights in the world" (Philippians 2:14-16).

Trust God. Why is it so hard to learn that God causes all things to work together for good to those who love God and are called according to His purpose? (Romans 8:28). My son and I were on the phone till the wee hours of the morning. He had played the first scrimmage and he said, "Dad, I was playing awesome. Dad, I'm not kidding. I mean, I had the seniors on the football team coming up to me and saying, 'Man, I didn't know you could play like that.' I was playing, Dad, and at the very last play, Dad, I went up to this guy and for whatever reason, I stopped." You never stop in a tackle, you drive through it. "I stopped and sprained my ankle."

With his voice cracking with pain, he said, "Why Dad? I went to camp and I worked with kids. I don't fool around, don't drink, don't do none of the stuff these guys are doing out there; but my ankle is busted and they have gone to play in Colorado. Why?"

I said, "Son, if God is for you, who can be against you? (Romans 8:31). Son, I'll tell you the truth, I am mad, too, but God never makes a mistake. And He always knows what He is doing. You are playing football to win a game and He is using football to develop character in you so that you will win in life not just a game."

"And not only this, but we also exult in our tribulations, knowing that tribulation brings about perseverance; and perseverance, proven character; and proven character, hope; and hope does not disappoint, because the love of God has been poured out within our hearts through the Holy Spirit who was given to us." (Romans 5:3-5)

I do want to emphasize once again that trusting God is a learning process (Proverbs 3:5-6). It is not something that comes automatically when you get saved. It is a continuous process. Yes, there are times when we do not understand all that is happening in our lives, but we must never stop trusting God.

Does that mean that we can never get troubled and frustrated? No! Do we question God? Yes! Did David get stressed out? Yes! Did Habakkuk wonder why? Yes! However, we must remember to question God as children question their father. Our anger should never lead us to turn our backs on God, quit praying, quit coming to church, or quit serving Him. That's when it has gone wrong.

Yes, you can get mad, you can cry, you can be frustrated, but just don't back away. Keep quoting verses. Learn to trust Him. It's a learned process. Just don't quit. By the way, before I left from my son's college dorm room I put up a poster. His mom likes to give him posters that keep him focused. So I put up this poster, which says, "A quitter is somebody who comes to the trial and fights the trial, but a person who wins goes through it." Learn not to fight the trial. Learn to make your way through the trial.

"Not that I speak from want, for I have learned to be content in whatever circumstances I am. I know how to get along with humble means, and I also know how to live in prosperity; in any and every circumstance I have learned the secret of being filled and going hungry, both of having abundance and suffering need. I can do all things through Him who strengthens me." (Philippians 4:11-13)

Always remember that you are never alone. Let us look once again at the temptations of Jesus. The Bible says that the Spirit led Jesus in the wilderness, which means Christ was led by the Holy Spirit. So was Christ alone? Meditate on these words. Was Christ alone? No! Well, I have great news for you. You are never alone. Satan wants you to think that you are alone. He wants you to believe that you are weak and lonely with no one to turn to. Don't ever think you're alone--because if you do, you fail. Hold on to this fact: you are never alone, God is always with you.

You should also know that you are not the only one who is facing temptations of various kinds. Remember Elijah? Think about it, God used the man in an awesome manner (1 Kings 18:37-39). I do understand how Elijah felt. I don't know why Mondays are not like Sundays. As a senior pastor, I prepare, pray, get my heart ready, get my mind ready, and get my spirit ready to be truly sincere to God on Sunday; because Monday is usually a low day for me. That is why I do not take off on Mondays.

Elijah had a wonderful time showing that God is great and then a woman named Jezebel comes along and Elijah takes off; running off to the mountains.

"I am alone, I am the only one who loves God. There is nobody for me. They are ready to beat me up and I just had to run up here and be by myself. I am just alone" (1 Kings 19:14).

Does God get mad at him? No! God understood his humanness. What did God say to him? "You're not alone. There are seven thousand people in Israel just like you" (1 Kings 19:15-18).

1 Peter 5:9 says, "But resist him (devil), firm in your faith, knowing that the same experiences of suffering are being accomplished by your brethren who are in the world." Remember this: Stay firm in the faith. In the midst of trials, don't complain about the trials, but stand firm. You are not going through your temptation alone.

As a senior pastor, God has used me to counsel many individuals, and I can tell you that there are many people who are facing the same temptations that you are facing today. Do you know why? Satan doesn't have new tricks. He is a created being who cannot come up with anything new. He tempts to hate and steal, kill and indulge in immorality, but he does not have new temptations! None! Therefore, if I'm going through something, and there are billions of people in the world, there are probably a lot of people going through the same thing. So never believe that you are alone.

America is a country of privacy. We lock our doors. We don't acknowledge our neighbors unless we are going to our car, and Satan says, "Good, keep it going, because if I can ever get you to think you're alone, I can destroy you." A wolf kills a sheep by separating it from its pack. Once the wolf singles out a sheep, you never see him continue chasing the pack. Instead the wolf runs after the sheep that has left the pack. But Jesus says, "I am with you always." The keyword in that sentence is *always*. "Even to the end of the age" (Matthew 28:20). Christ has provided ministering angels to guard us (Psalm 34:7; Hebrews 1:14). Trust Him!

Consider Fasting. Another step towards overcoming temptation involves fasting. Do you remember when the disciples commanded the demon to come out of a person? What did Christ say? "But this kind does not go out except by prayer and fasting" (Matthew 17:21).

In other words, there are times when we are tested and we feel like we are cracking. When that happens, it's time to deny the basic needs that we have, and say, "God, I know that you are all-powerful. Your strength is all I need to overcome my temptation." Think about it for a minute, Jesus was hungry in the wilderness, but His hunger did not drive Him away from His Father. His hunger helped Him to focus on God, because as a human being, it created a greater level of dependence on God. The decision to fast must rest on the Word of God and must be accompanied with prayer.

My son teases me and says, "Dad, you really don't know when to turn something off at the stove, do you? Every time you cook, something is burnt."

I said, "Son, I have a hard time figuring when it's cooked on the inside. So I figure if it is black on the outside, it has to be brown on the inside."

Sometimes we want to stop cooking when the outside looks good, without realizing it has not finished cooking on the inside. God wants you cooked on the inside and when you're cooked on the inside and full of the Holy Spirit that you will be able to overcome your temptation. Jesus, who defeated the purposes of Satan and rose from the grave, declares, "All authority has been given to Me in heaven and on earth." (Matthew 28:18) When you make Jesus the Lord of your life, temptations will not be able to overwhelm or overcome you.

Every single day God pours out the sun. Every single day He keeps the earth spinning. Every breath we take is a gift from God. Every blessing we enjoy comes from the Lord (James 1:17). You are able to read this book by the grace of the Almighty. So what is stopping us from running to Jesus? When we turn to Jesus, the outside circumstances will no longer be able to control our lives.

Temptations are tough and you never know how long they are going to last, but take your steps to faith. Victory can be yours—reach out and claim it as directed by the power of the Lord through His written Word.

CHAPTER 2

Living through Adversity

So it came about, when Joseph reached his brothers, that they stripped Joseph of his tunic, the varicolored tunic that was on him, and they took him and threw him into the pit. Now the pit was empty, without any water in it. Then they sat down to eat a meal. Genesis (37:23-25)

There is a story told about two trees in a garden. The oak tree had been in the garden for many years, but the other tree was struggling to survive. However, both the trees were facing the same storms that came through that particular town.

As the story goes, the younger tree got tired of seeing this oak tree standing strong, so it said, "Old oak tree."

The oak tree answered, "Yes, what do you want?"

The other tree said, "How do you make it through the difficult times when life is so rough? Your roots are not pulled out, your leaves are not falling off the way mine are and your branches are not broken. How are you making it?"

The oak tree replied, "Well, storms will come, but I am structured in such a way that my roots are bent around the rocks and I am able to weather the storms."

There is not a person alive today that has not gone through or is going through storms in life. When pain grips your heart and body; when sorrow overwhelms you; when you are the recipient of one bad news after the other; do you wonder why God does not remove from us the struggles and difficulties that come from life? The Bible tells us that tribulations, hardships, and difficulties will come (John 16:33).

I recently spent the day with one of my sons in Weatherford, Oklahoma. I came back with a heavy heart and was talking to my wife when she said, "What do you want to do? Do you want to spare him from the difficulties of being hurt so that he becomes all that he wants to be without adversity? Or do you want him to go through it so that God doesn't just build a great student, He builds a great man?"

Some people walk away from God because they believe that a good God must not allow adversities to come their way. If everyone that became saved, never became ill; instead, became exceedingly rich, received promotions, got the best jobs available, drove the best cars, lived in the best houses, with God removing all the troublesome people from their lives, and then wiped out all the consequences of every wrong action they have taken, who wouldn't be saved? Who would they miss in the process? JESUS! The only reason that these people would come to Him is to reap the prosperity that comes from being saved. They would come to Jesus Christ for what they could get from Him.

God loves you and He understands your sorrow and your pain. Even in the midst of your adversity, if you truly start counting the blessings in your life, you will realize the goodness of God. God does not want to be like a Santa Claus in your life. Christ wants to teach you what life is all about. He is building you for His kingdom. He is preparing you for eternity. God's love and grace was sufficient for Joseph to live through his adversity. His love and grace is available to you so you can live through yours.

Jesus and Suffering

Jesus Christ Himself did not live in the greatest mansion that He could find while He was on earth. He was not born into a family that was rich. In fact, the Bible says that He had no place to lay His head. Christ could tell folks how to find money in the mouth of a fish! He could tell Peter where to go fishing to get the best fish, but He did not live filthy rich when He could have done so. The One who is Omnipotent could have commanded anything, at anytime, but He chose to live through adversity. In the entire duration of His life on earth, He lived through one calamity after another. The religious leaders hated Him, Judas betrayed Him, and He died nailed to a cross.

God Cares—Do you?

Jesus loves you so much that He gave His life for you. When you are facing adversity, remember you have a High Priest who listens to and understands the very groans of your hearts. You don't have a "don't care, God" who doesn't concern Himself with your struggles. Hebrews 4:15 talks about, "For we do not have a High Priest who cannot sympathize with our weaknesses, but One who has been tempted in all things as we are, yet without sin." The word sympathy means that God is willing to come to you and walk with you in the midst of your adversities. He feels the very pain you are going through. He feels your hurt, your anxiety, your struggles, and when you pray, He is your true intercessor. Rejoice, because you don't have an unconcerned God.

You may have some friends who will feel sorry for you during your adversity, but they may not be able to help you overcome your adversity. You may have other friends who may join you in the gutter and make your adversity worse. The knowledge that you and I have of Jesus the King always excites me. And the King says, "I sympathize with you, because I can be down in the gutter and I can be up on the bank. You need me in the gutter so I can share your pain, your hardships and your difficulties. But you also need me on the bank so that I can get you out of the gutter and guide you toward truth and light." (Hebrews 4:15)

Now that we have established that God cares about those who are suffering, it would be pertinent to ask if we care about others. The difficulty with people going through struggles is that they can't find Christians who are concerned with their struggles. The problem is not that we have an unconcerned God; the problem is finding people who love God so much that they would show concern for His people. We're too busy with this world's affairs to ever be concerned enough to slow down and turn off the television long enough to take the time to listen.

God cares, do you?

My Personal Story

As a youngster, I remember Sister Clark teaching us during our discipleship class that the best thing to pray for is wisdom. She also taught us that God is going to help us gain wisdom by taking us through trials. At the age of thirteen, I went home and I prayed, "God, I don't know what is up in front of me, but I pray for wisdom tonight." I asked the Lord to give me wisdom like Solomon.

Well, life has not been an easy journey for me. I remember when I was 16 and used to run to work for $1.60/hour with my hands in my pocket, because it was freezing cold and I had no jacket. My wife and I experienced days when there was no food on the table, we were not sure if we were going to make it to the next day, the kids were sick and needed surgery, and there was no money. Through it all God never left us alone. I learned the important principles of life as God taught me to apply His Word through adversity. These lessons of life remain so precious to me, because they drew me close to my Savior in a powerful way. I have come to understand that trials are painful, but we can learn to apply His Scriptures to life through times of adversity.

Believe in Your Heart

If you read the life story of Joseph, notice that the author repeatedly confirms, "the Lord was with Joseph." The Lord did not speak with a special voice to Joseph declaring, "I am with you now, just keep going." There is no place in this passage where God spoke to Joseph and said in a unique manner, "I am here." Joseph believed in his heart that God would not forsake him and God was always with him. You have to believe in your heart that God will never forsake you.

During the most difficult times in my life--my wife will tell you--I would say, "God will not bring us this far and leave us. I don't believe that I have a God that would do that to me." However, I do know how emotions can go wild during adversity. There are times when you feel like crying and days when you feel so lonely you want to give up. There are times when you do not know what to do. "For I am convinced that neither death, nor life, nor angels, nor principalities, nor things present, nor things to come, nor powers, nor height, nor depth, nor any other created thing, shall be able to separate us from the love of God, which is in Christ Jesus our Lord" (Romans 8: 38-39)

Nothing will separate you from the love of God. I believe that Daniel believed that God was present with him when he was thrown into the lion's den. David stood in front of Goliath, a nine-foot tall experienced warrior, because he believed that God was with him. Does this mean that you will never falter? No! Elijah ran off to a mountain after having a wonderful time with the priests of Balaam. The great men of faith did not necessarily have great faith every single moment. However, when they chose to believe in God's word at a particular time, in a particular place, God came through for them powerfully. Your circumstances may be harsh, but hold on to this fact, God will never forsake you and God does not lie.

Abide in Him

I know what it is like to sit in a dorm room with 14 stitches across my eyes, bruised ribs, sprained wrist, and without a dime in my pocket, but to keep going to school. I know what it is like to get a note saying that if I don't pay my tuition by Monday morning, I will be kicked out of school all in one weekend. I know what it feels like to walk out of my room to check my mail just to see if something wonderful will happen in the next second and nothing changes. I know what it is like to go back to my dorm room and sit there not getting a call, not hearing from anybody, not knowing how I am going to make it.

I also know that God wants me to love Him. Love Him? We take that lightly. In order to love Him, we must keep His commandments. The problem is getting outside of His purpose and His Word, and expecting God, in the midst of adversity, to stay with us. He does not neglect us in terms of salvation, but He cannot abide with us during those times that we are living outside of His Word. He abides with us, because we obey His Word and abide in Him.

Jesus wants you to know that He will never leave you. He will never let you out of His salvation plan, but you will not experience His power if you don't stay faithful in the midst of the struggle. Abide in Him and you will receive the nourishment you need to journey through your adversity.

Hold on to His Word

If you're jumping out of a plane, you don't cut off the parachute cords because you fell out. You don't say, "I'm sick of this. This person pushed me out to teach me how to parachute and I don't feel like it." You don't do that, you hold on to the parachute harder!

I remember while in Freeport Bahamas, my son talked me into parasailing. That thing took me up so high, I said, "Lord if you bring me back I'll love you more!" I asked the guy when I landed, "Just suppose that rope broke? Would that parachute bring me down pretty good?" He said, "No, it's not designed for that. You'll come down like a rock, pretty much. You'll die." Thanks for telling me that when I got back!

I learned what it is like to be up there and when I was up there, I was not about to let go of anything. I held on to that thing. You could have told me, "Man, let go, it's going to be okay. You can do all kinds of tricks up there. If you let go, you can spin and catch the thing. You can flip and catch." Well, I was not interested in tricks. I was not interested in anything but holding on.

We must never let go of God's Word. When you go through uncomfortable spots, trials, doubts, questions, don't let go of His Word. The Word of God is powerful and is sharper then a double edged sword (Hebrews 4:12). That's our power! The Holy Spirit came to guide us in the truth and to teach us the truth. That's awesome power! We can not let go of the power. "In the beginning was the Word, and the Word was with God, and the Word was God" (John 1:1). Jesus is the Word. That's Him who loves you, so don't let go of Him.

Serve Him Faithfully

During times of adversity, every chore becomes drudgery. However, I want to challenge you to serve God faithfully wherever He places you. I don't care if it is mopping floors; I don't care if it is climbing up and cutting down trees. Wherever God places you, and as long as He places you there, serve Him there faithfully. When we are willing to be faithful in a few things, God blesses us with more.

Joseph--you would think this man would be mad at God. You would think that Joseph's adversity lasted for a year. Oh no! Joseph's ordeal lasted for 13 long years. It wasn't a one-year or two-year deal; it wasn't like Joseph became a prince when he turned 18. No, his adversity took 13 years! His brothers turned their backs on him and decided that they would put him in a well. In fact, they were going to kill him if it wasn't for Reuben. They threw him in the well and then sat down to eat a meal. That's cold-blooded.

Joseph was sold to the Ishmaelites and bought by Potiphar, an Egyptian officer of Pharaoh and the captain of the bodyguard. Do you think Potiphar came to Joseph and said, "Oh Joseph, you look great. I'm going to go ahead and promote you?" No! We don't know how long Joseph worked in Potiphar's house before he was promoted. In the 13-year period of time, he could have worked in this man's house for two to three years, not hearing from his father or his brothers, not knowing if he will ever have a better life. He was in Egypt and probably did not have a clue as to how to get home. Alone, deserted, neglected, and rejected--but he was faithful to what God had called him to do.

Whether he was at Potiphor's house, in the jail cell, or at the palace, Joseph served the Lord faithfully.

God can't promote some of us, because we're fussing about what He wants us to do now by saying, "I'm sick of this life. I am bored taking care of mundane chores every day. Don't even let it rain on the wrong day. If I wash my car today, Lord, will you wait until next week for it to rain?" And God is saying, "I need to test your heart. Are you going to be faithful doing what I have placed in your hands now?"

Joseph didn't complain when there wasn't anything coming from heaven. There was no church to encourage him. Nothing! He didn't quit. Here is a man who was thrown into prison through no fault of his own. Was Joseph fighting, arguing, or even cursing? It is not like the man put him in prison and said, "You got two years." It is not like the man put him in prison and said, "You have a year, you have five months." He just put him in prison with no time period. How would you like to be thrown in the prison and not told when you are getting out? Why do you think the judge tells when one is going to get out? To give hope! But Joseph is not given any hope. Nothing! The man just put him in jail and leaves him there. Yet what does Joseph do? He stays faithful.

Galatians 6:9-10 says. "Let us not lose heart in doing good, for in due time we shall reap." In due time is however long it takes to go through the hard times. For Joseph, it took him thirteen years of staying faithful to God. In due time we will reap: "if we do not grow weary, so then while we have opportunity." That means while there is time, while we are alive and breathing, not only while things are good and perfect and wonderful. "Let us do good to all men, and especially to those who are of the household of faith." Watch out especially for Christian brothers and sisters. If you cannot do good for folks that sit right next to you in the pews, then it is going to be hard for you to do it for folks outside.

When I was a youth minister at Oak Cliff Bible Fellowship in Dallas, Texas, I would come up with some of the greatest plans because an old preacher had taught me, "Paul it doesn't matter what vineyard God puts you in. Whatever vineyard He puts you in, that's the vineyard you serve Him in. You don't serve men, you serve God."

The joy of serving God is overwhelmingly greater than you can imagine. Be faithful to God wherever He puts you. If you think your husband does not have any sense, learn to be the wife God called you to be, period. If you think your wife is not half way there, you learn to be what a husband is designed to be biblically. As a single parent, learn to be a good parent to your child. If you are single, learn to be a great single person. In everything, know that He has called you and has set the race before you, so serve Him faithfully.

Joseph did not mess with God's plan. He never said, "God, why did you send me here? I have no hope." Joseph did not figure out until much later in his life that his adversity was leading to the salvation of his people. He would have never figured that out if he had given up in Egypt, tried to commit suicide, jumped off a bridge, or become bitter and vengeful. Joseph remained faithful and he saw that God had a marvelous plan for his life.

Faithfulness Produces Trust

Adversity cannot be used as an excuse for unfaithfulness. Remember faithfulness will always produce trust. Some of us can't be trusted; you have to be trusted. If your boss tells you to be there at 8:00 A. M., be there; your boss does not need to call and check. If your boss tells you to write something down on a piece of paper; do it and do it with excellence, because you represent the love of Christ on your job.

If your spouse says something and you don't feel like doing it, you don't slam the doors saying, "I'll do it." You share the love of God even as you fulfill your duties at home. You're beating God's kingdom plan if you start messing with His plan. You don't know what it does to your children when they watch you love your husband or when they watch you love your wife. When they watch you maintain your purity, you don't know what that does to that child. You don't know what that does to another generation, and it could go on for generations because we chose to be faithful and worthy of trust despite our adversity.

Maintain Your Integrity—Do not Violate God's Trust

Joseph was a man with extraordinary good looks and his boss' wife started checking him out. She was not bashful about checking him out either. She looks at him with desire and says to him, "Lie with me" (Genesis 39:7). Now that's bold. She was bold and she did not feel guilty about it.

Joseph could have used the situation to his advantage. "Well, she is the boss. If she commands me

I just have to agree to it." He could have been like Abraham. God had told Abraham that his wife is going to have his child. If he had held on to God's Word he would not have slept with Haggar, but he says, "You know Sarah, you have a point!"

Not Joseph! Joseph refused, but do you think she quit? No! The woman nagged the brother to death. Day after day Joseph was nagged, nagged, and nagged. Day after day--you may go to work and a person enrages you. Satan just nags you to death. He wants you to break and fall apart. He is going to nag you. He is going to keep throwing it at you. "I am alone; no one loves me; maybe I deserve some happiness. My adversity is driving me crazy and God needs to understand my pain." Nag, nag, and nag some more.

Joseph refused and said, "My master has put all that he owns in my charge. How could I violate that trust? The only thing he held back is you because you are his wife" (Genesis 39: 8-9). He uses the word, wife, and not woman. Wife! "You belong to him, wife. I know that God would never let me touch another man's wife."

Integrity is maintained because you respect the trust that you gained. You make it through adversity because God has entrusted to you your car, your home, your education, indeed your very life. He's entrusted that to you. You cannot violate His trust. All good things come from above folks, all good things. You don't have that house because you just have that house. You have that house because God has entrusted it to you. You can't violate his trust. You have that pay check because God has entrusted it to you. God has granted to you all good things and you cannot violate His trust.

So Joseph says, "I cannot sin against God" (Genesis 39:9). You would think he would say, "I cannot sin against your husband." No. "I cannot sin against God." Unless Christians recognize that, they will not be prepared to take any steps to faith. As long as we look at the issues in life attached to a person, attached to an issue, attached to somebody on the job, attached to somebody in the household, we will never make it through adversity.

The Bible says that you do not wrestle against flesh and blood. You wrestle with principalities and powers of this dark world and against the spiritual forces of evil (Ephesians 6:12). If you're going through struggles and hardships, it is not just the other person or the situation that you are dealing with, it is Satan and he is coming against you. God is going to test the sincerity, commitment, and integrity of your heart as you learn to live through your adversity. Do not violate His trust even if your whole world is falling apart.

My son came home one day and said, "In practice I run the ball faster, but this guy keeps standing in front of me." I said, "Son, you got a major problem." He said, "I don't have a problem, the coach does, Dad." I said, "No, he doesn't, you got it." He sat down on the couch and looked at me like I had lost my mind. I said, "Son, until you fight, you, you will always grow to the other guy's level. If there's anything I learned in sports is that you never look at the other person and compare yourself with him to determine how good you will be. You look at you own potential and determine from your own potential the achievements you can make."

We have to peek over the wall of the person that is with us or the person that is against us. We have to peek over that wall and look at what God is trying to do in us and through us. Until then, we will never live through adversity. It is not about flesh and blood, it is spiritual warfare. Learn to say with Joseph, "I will not sin against my God."

Faithfulness in Adversity leads to Blessings

Faithfulness will lead to God promoting you in due season. How do I know that? The Bible tells us that Joseph's master saw that the Lord was with him and the Lord caused all that he did to prosper in his hand. So the master made Joseph in charge of everything. In fact, we are repeatedly told that Joseph managed everything. When the Bible repeats something, it is trying to make a point. Joseph had everything. He could do whatever he wanted. He walked to work anytime he wanted to go to work and left whenever he wanted to leave. The man trusted Joseph. He didn't even ask Joseph how the checkbook looked. He didn't care to find out anything. That is some promotion (Genesis 39: 3-6).

A commitment to God in the midst of adversity leads to great blessings. Joseph is promoted because he did not sin when his brothers put him in the well. He did not try to kill them. He just kept working where he was and you know what that produced. No matter where he went God kept his promotion. I like that. I like people promoted by God. Do you know why? Because when God promotes you, circumstances and people will never be able to take away that promotion. Somebody could move you to something else, but God is going to keep you promoted. Somebody could move you someplace else, but God is going to hold your family together. You could be broke and out of work and God is the one that's going to make your wife not worry about anything and just hold on to you. Your situation as a single person may get rough, but God will keep you promoted.

Joseph switched jobs and he was still in charge of everything. That's a man of God. You switch jobs and stay at the top. Joseph is the first man I know that had problems with his clothing. He had on a bright coat that got him in a well. He had on a jacket; a woman kept it and put him in jail. His clothes just keep getting him in trouble, but God kept him promoted. So get your promotion from God and nobody will be able to tear you down. They will come at you in adversity. They can pull at you; they can come after your job; they may come after your husband; your wife; they can come after your children; but God will keep you promoted.

Remain Faithful Despite Your Blessings

Joseph remained faithful to God despite his blessings. You may think that when Joseph became Pharaoh's man he said, "Oh, you all coming for food, huh. I know who you are. You are dead. God blessed me and brought you right to me. Dream has come true. I am going to kill you."

However, Joseph's promotion did not cause him to lose his mind. Some folks get promoted and they get arrogant. They get out of their car and walk right by you. You talk about giving when they're making more money? No. Ten percent of $50,000 a year is too much. That's why God keeps some of us at $25,000 a year or $15,000 a year. Just like the man who was making $30,000; but he was willing to give ten percent to the Lord. The preacher prayed for him and he got promoted to a six-figure job, and he says, "Man, I am struggling with giving." The preacher got up and said, "God, would you please take him back to $30,000!"

Joseph did not get arrogant. He was promoted in Potiphar's house and he served faithfully. He was promoted in the jail cell and he served faithfully. God created a situation; allowed him to be promoted, and Pharaoh put his signet ring on him. Here's a man that's a Hebrew. The Egyptians hated Hebrews. God took a hated man and made him ruler over all the other people and Joseph continued to serve faithfully.

Joseph kept a humble spirit even when his brothers who had tried to destroy him showed up. In fact, he said some very profound and thoughtful words, "God sent me before you to preserve you for a remnant in the earth, and to keep you alive by a great deliverance. Hurry and go up to my father, and say to him, 'Thus says your son Joseph, God has made me lord of all Egypt; come down to me, do not delay.' And you shall live in the land of Goshen, and you shall be near me, you and your children and your children's children and your flocks and your herds and all that you have" (Genesis 45:7, 9-10).

Read this carefully; God fights the proud. Nebuchadnezzar was promoted, but when he became arrogant God made him eat grass for seven years. David was a man after God's own heart and God promoted him; but he decided – she is cute and I am going to make her mine. David's promotion elevated his brain to arrogance and God had to bring him down to where this great king had to sneak out of the backside of the city. When God decides to bring your adversity to an end and blesses you, thank Him and praise His name and get His vision to help you see through you. Don't let blessings corrupt you. God wants to bless you, but He will bless you in His time and in a manner that He knows is best for you. Remember He does not want to just bless you with things, He wants to bless you with a fine character.

I do not know how long your adversity is going to last—it may last for two weeks, 10 years, or even 13 years. I do not know and I am not going to tell you that I know. I do know that if you follow the above principles as you live through your adversity, in due season, God will raise you up. I say this with such confidence, because I know that you can do all things through Christ who strengthens you (Philippians 4:13). You are more than a conqueror. In the words of the Psalmist: "Why are you in despair, O my soul? And why have you become disturbed within me? Hope in God, for I shall again praise Him for the help of His presence" (Psalm 42:5). God has never failed me during my trials and I know that He will never fail you as you take your steps to faith even as you go through your adversities.

Hold His hand and let Him lead you!

CHAPTER 3

Dealing with Hopelessness

Jesus wept. And so the Jews were saying, "Behold how He loved Him!" But some of them said, "Could not this man, who opened the eyes of him who was blind, have kept this man also from dying?" (John 11:35-36)

Have you tried everything but failed in life? Are you being accused of something you did not commit? Do you believe that no one understands the depth of your pain and sorrow? Have you been thrown out of your job and you do not have the energy to look for another one? Were you hoping that the new medication will work but the infection continues to spread to other parts of your body? Were you waiting for a miracle for your loved ones but death came and stole them away? Perhaps you are so lonely that you find it hard to smile. Let me put it another way: Are you experiencing hopelessness today?

According to a journal of medicine 20 percent of the people that die from hardened arteries, suffer death because they live without hope. People who live without hope can harm their health as much as those who smoke a pack of cigarettes a day.

In fact, soldiers that give up hope are the first to die in prison camps. They come to a point where they just sit in their waste and do not care about anything. They are told that they will be shot and it does not bother them since they believe that life has no hope to offer them.

There is something sinister about the word, "hopelessness." It has a ring of desperation around it; bringing along a feeling of desolation. Hopelessness sinks in when everything fails. Hopelessness comes when all expectations are destroyed. Hopelessness springs from seemingly impossible situations. Oh, hopelessness can be deadly.

Most of us experience some level of hopelessness at some point or another in our lives. It may come through different scenarios for various individuals, but it always results in desperation and despondency.

During such tumultuous moments, our hearts cry out, and we begin to question--What should one do when hopelessness strikes? Is there any hope in the midst of hopelessness? Does God have an answer for our hopelessness?

Struggling with Hopelessness

Mary and Martha experienced hopelessness. They came to a point in their lives when they honestly believed that all hope was lost. If you have read the biblical account, you know that Jesus loved Mary, Martha, and their brother, Lazarus. John tells us that when Lazarus fell sick, his sisters immediately sent a message to Jesus saying, "Lord, behold, he whom you love is sick." (John 11:3)

Do you remember a time in your life when you were hit by a storm, but your faith was strong and you believed that the problem was going to be solved? You expected the storm to last for some time, but you did not doubt God's love for you. You expected God to respond to your message. Mary and Martha knew that Jesus had the power to heal the sick and they expected Him to respond to their message.

However, Jesus continues to stay in the place where He was for two more days (John 11:6) and Lazarus dies. While Lazarus was sick, Mary and Martha could pray for a miracle. When Lazarus dies, they have to deal with hopelessness.

Jesus Meets You at Your Point of Need

Jesus meets Mary and Martha at their point of need. When your "Lazarus" dies, and your world is breaking down, remember that Jesus will meet you at your point of need. Never forget that. What is your need? What is causing hopelessness in your life? Allow Christ to meet you at your point of need and restore hope in your life again.

You may say, "I am waiting, but there is no sign of Jesus meeting me during my time of need. I cry and beg, but He does not respond." You may say like the Jews, "Could not Jesus who opened the eyes of blind people, who raised a dead man, answer my cries for help?"

When storms come in my life, I don't take them lightly. I don't believe that anything happens by accident. Rather, I believe that things happen so we can learn from them. Sometimes it seems like God is not answering because we want Him to respond the way we want, according to our timing. We forget that God has a wonderful plan for our lives and His timing is perfect.

Christ knew that Lazarus was dead and had already planned what He was going to do while they were sweating.

Mary and Martha said, "He's sick, come help Lazarus."

Christ says, "No, you don't need me right now. You need me when it is time for me to help you and God to be glorified."

Mary and Martha believed that Jesus had the power to raise their brother from sickness. "Lord, if you had been here, my brother would not have died" (John 11:21, 32). Their knowledge of Jesus was limited, and they expected Jesus to respond according to their knowledge.

If you read further, "Jesus said, 'Remove the stone.'

Martha, the sister of the deceased said to Him, "Lord by this time there will be stench, for he has been dead four days." (John 11:39)

Even after talking to Jesus, Martha was unable to comprehend that nothing is impossible for Jesus. Like Martha, there are times when we limit God to what we know about Him. We bring up our rotting situations and confine God's abilities to what we believe He can do.

And then Jesus said to her, "Did I not say to you, if you believe you will see the glory of God?" (John 11:40) Jesus' response tells us that even when our faith is shaky, He will meet us at our point of need and walk with us.

If Jesus had granted Mary and Martha's request, Lazarus would have received physical healing, but Jesus would have remained just a great Healer for them. However, Jesus delayed His trip and taught an eternal truth--not only to the sisters, but also to all the generations to come--that He is the resurrection and the life (John 11:25).

He is Christ, the Son of God, and the Lord of the universe. Jesus came at a time when they had no hope; and Mary and Martha witnessed a miracle that was beyond their imagination. God wants to respond to your hopelessness. Wait for His plan and His timing and you will be amazed at the answer you receive.

Come to Jesus

Jesus requires that you come. When you are faced with hopelessness, Jesus says, "Come to me." You see Christ did not come into the village (Matthew 11:28-30). He never made it to the village. He stayed two miles outside, because He needed them to come to Him so that He could do what He wanted to do. Sometimes you may ask--why does God let a situation get so bad? Christ says He needs you to believe. He needs you to see that no matter how difficult, hard, or how pressing a situation is, He can deliver you. He wants us to come to Him.

I hadn't had a chance to go to the gym in a while. When I eventually decided to go, I tried to lift the same weight that I had lifted the last time I was there. I pushed; not really going very far. If the first one is that hard, you have to change the weight.

After I finished changing the weight, a guy came right behind me, muscles showing and all that, took the pin and put it all the way back down to the bottom. He lifted all that weight with such ease and comfort that I wanted to forsake the gym and run.

Sometimes our sorrows weigh so much that we do not have the strength to lift them. Sometimes it feels that the weight of our misfortunes will crush us to death. Jesus sees our struggles and says, "I have the power to remove the weights from your life. Come to me."

What is the best thing to do when people are hurting? Go to the hospital and sit by them. Am I right? Go to their house and take a meal, right? This is not what Jesus does. He goes and sits two miles outside of the village and makes those women run, because no matter when Jesus comes, He still expects us to express our faith. Although Jesus is coming, He still requires that we come.

"Come" in the Bible is not a passive word. "Come" means to keep moving, like a two-year old active child always running; or the woman who lost her coin and tore up her house trying to look for her coin. It says, "I cannot find an answer to this problem, but I am still going to reach out to you." It's like moving when someone tells you there are a million dollars waiting for you on the coffee table. It does not matter how much traffic is backed up; you are going to find a way to that table.

"Come" is like having a 65% off sale on a Saturday morning before a certain time. I will never forget the day my wife woke me early in the morning so that we could get to an apple day sale to pick up

Dealing with Hopelessness **43**

some school clothes for our children. She got her coupons and when we walked into the store; there were people everywhere trying to pull things off the racks as if it was some kind of a raid. Indeed, "come" makes me think of an insistent person who refuses to stop until Jesus restores.

Come as you are. You don't have to change your personality to go to Jesus. He never asks you to put aside your pain when you go to Him. If you are hurting, Jesus doesn't ask you to stop hurting. If you are crying, He doesn't tell you to stop crying. If you do not have the strength for words, He does not expect you to give a speech. Jesus wants you to come as you are.

Were people running behind Martha when she ran out of the house? No one ran after her. Martha goes out and everyone just sat there (John 11:20). Mary goes out and everyone ran behind her (John 11:31). Did Jesus say, "Mary, you are the more popular one, so I'll wait for you. Martha, you go back, you are not hurting like Mary. In fact, you are handling this pretty good." Martha did not cry.. It is not recorded anywhere in the passage that Martha cried. She wanted to discuss why He did not come when He received the message. That's Martha. She wanted a rational explanation and Jesus gave her an intellectual response. Mary came weeping and Christ wept with her.

When I say that Jesus meets you at your point of need; it does not mean that when He comes you must be prepared to have a theological discourse and know your doctrines well. Jesus says, "If you want to have a conversation with me or argue with me, I will argue with you. If you want to cry, I will cry with you. You don't have to fix it to come; you just come."

Some people cannot come to Him when they are hurting, because they do not want others to know that they are hurting. Some believe that Jesus will only accept them if they come to Him in a specific manner. However, I have learned that Jesus Christ does not expect me to come to Him in a certain posture, position, or with specific words. Many of us are always trying to fix and plan the way we come, while all the time He is saying, come—just as you are.

When you come to Jesus. You can come to Jesus in prayer. Tell Him everything that's on your heart. He is your Father and you can share your sorrows with Him. Even if the whole world chooses to misunderstand you, He understands what you are going through and He cares. Do you know that every time you pray, you come to Jesus? Prayer opens a wonderful channel of communication with your Friend, who is also your Lord.

Another way to "come" is through His Word. Search through His Word and find out what it says about your particular situation. Are you dealing with grief and sorrow? Find out what His Word says. Do you have a burden that is overwhelming you? Galatians 6:2 says, "Bear one another's burdens, and thus fulfill the law of Christ." Find a godly person with whom you can talk, interact, and share your pain. Is there any particular issue that is confusing you? Search for answers in the Bible and you will be able to say with the Psalmist, "Thy word is a lamp to my feet, and a light to my path" (Psalm 119:105).

There was a little boy who fell down and bruised his knee. People came running to the boy, because it looked like his knee was badly messed up. They surrounded the child who was screaming and hollering.

Dealing with Hopelessness **45**

They tried to help him up, but the boy could hardly move. When he saw his mother running down the street, the little boy popped up and ran to his mother, crying, "Momma, momma, momma". He grabbed his mother and they hugged and cried together. The little boy went home sniffling, but walking.

When you run to Jesus, you declare that you believe that He cares. The child did not think, "Oh, my mother is not a doctor." The child ran and grabbed his mother, trusting that she loved him. He did not waste his time doubting or questioning. You come to Jesus because you believe. You know that He loves you. Your knowledge translates into action when you run towards Him, trusting Him, because you know that He wants you to come to Him.

Jesus Identifies with Your Struggles

"Jesus wept." (John 11:35) When Jesus saw Mary and the Jews who came with her weeping; He was deeply moved in spirit and He wept. Please understand that these words are picked out to show us how much God cares when we hurt. John makes it clear that Jesus was deeply moved in spirit. He wants you to know that Jesus feels the pain you feel in the midst of your grief. Yes, He feels the pain you feel during your difficult times.

When we understand how God loves us and how He responds to our needs, we will not allow ourselves to get wiped out by this life's worries and cares. Hebrews 2:17 says, "Therefore, He (Jesus) had to be made like His brethren (human) in all things, that He might become a merciful and faithful High Priest in all things pertaining to God, to make propitiation for the sins of the people. For since He Himself was tempted (tested) in that which He has suffered, He is able to come to the aid of those who are tempted."

Jesus knows what it means to be ridiculed and rejected. He understands hunger and discomfort. He Himself was despised and forsaken. He has been described as a man of sorrows and acquainted with grief. (Isaiah 53:3) He was oppressed and He was afflicted, yet He did not open His mouth. (Isaiah 53:7) He was cut off out of the land of the living and His grave was assigned with wicked men. (Isaiah 53:8-9)

Jesus understands and He comes to our help. Jesus Christ says, "I can come to your aid in any situation because I have experienced everything that you are going through, have gone through, or are going to go through." Mary went crying to Jesus. Weeping in the Jewish community meant she was literally hollering. Mary did not come sniffling; she came hollering and screaming. Jesus did not say, "Mary, behave yourself!" Jesus wept with her.

God is never too busy for you and He will never walk away when you need Him. He also loves you so much that He identifies with your every struggle and He will be with you until the end of time.

Jesus Is Able To Solve Problems

Jesus never weeps without hope. Jesus cried intensely with Mary, but He did not cry without hope. Although Jesus Christ identifies with your struggles, He weeps with hope, because He knows He can fix it. Jesus raised Lazarus four days after his death and decomposition had set in. In those days, it was believed that the spirit hovered around the body for three days. After the third day, when the body did not respond, the spirit would go to heaven. Jesus Christ put an end to that myth after He raised Lazarus from the grave. What power and authority belongs to Jesus!

Perhaps you are thinking Lazarus was raised, but you are still waiting for God to raise your loved ones. Well, Lazarus eventually died, and all of us are going to end our journey on earth some day. However, when we die, it is not that our spirits will become light-weighted and float through the sky. The great news for a Christian is that when we die, Jesus Himself, who is the Resurrection and the Life, will come and usher our spirits to heaven. Indeed, what power and authority belongs to Jesus! The God of all ages holds not only your past and present, but also your future in His hands. So come, confess in the midst of your hopelessness that Jesus has the ability to solve all your problems.

The other day I was standing at the airport counter, getting ready to get on a plane. I heard the pilot talking to the airline personnel. The pilot was told that although the necessary checks had not taken place, the plane was scheduled to depart in five minutes. The pilot said, "We are going to be late." The personnel said, "We have to go." The pilot responded firmly, "You know, I have a family too!" I can never forget those words. That was some pilot.

When we are standing at the counters of grief, hardship, and financial difficulties, we just want to take off. Nevertheless, Christ is saying: "Hold on! It is important to learn to fly, but it is equally important to learn to land safely. Be patient and wait until I accomplish all the checks in your life." God is never in a hurry and He is never late. He wants to fix your circumstances, but He does not want you to only experience the joy of your flight. He wants to make sure that you have a safe landing, too.

Desperate times have a way of making us feel helpless. As long as we live on this earth, we will experience storms that seem to have the potential to drown us in hopelessness. Indeed, Satan wants to take every part of our life and ravish us with worries and cares so that we will give up on God. Nevertheless, the Bible says that the joy of the Lord will be your strength (Nehemiah 8:10).

How can a child of God, torn and ripped apart by storms, hope to experience the joy of the Lord? One can experience the joy of the Lord when you commit your hopes, dreams, and frustrations in the hands of the Almighty King. When you are willing to rest beneath His wings, you can say, "His grace is sufficient, for His power is perfected in your weakness." (2 Corinthians 12:9) His grace is sufficient for every hopeless situation of yours; especially when things are not working out the way you wanted them to and you are hurting really bad. I know that there will come a time when He will meet you and raise you from your "Lazarus" situation. He will remove all wrappings from your hands and feet and face (John 11:44) and He will set you free.

Jesus said to Martha (and He is saying to you), "I am the resurrection and the life; he who believes in me shall live even if he dies, and everyone who lives and believes in me shall never die. Do you believe this?" (John 11:25-26)

Faith in Jesus will lead you to confidence in your life. When all else fails, remember Christ cares.

CHAPTER 4

Guilty, but not Condemned

And the Scribes and the Pharisees brought a woman caught in adultery, and having set her in the midst, they said to Him, "Teacher, this woman has been caught in adultery, in the very act. Now in the Law, Moses commanded us to stone such women; what then do you say? (John 8:3-5)

There is not a person alive who can say," I have no sin." You may say, "I am a good person. I don't lie, I don't cheat, I don't drink, I don't smoke, I am not on drugs, I don't fool around. I don't do this; I don't do that." But being a good person does not mean that you have no sin in you. The First Epistle of John says, "If we say that we have no sin, we are deceiving ourselves, and the truth is not in us" (1 John 1:8).

It is not good to sin. There are consequences to sinning. Our relationship with God suffers when we sin. God sometimes causes us to lose our position or wealth. We may face difficulties in our lives because of sin. In fact, if we come to the Lord's Supper in an unworthy manner, we are held guilty before God. If we do not correct it, some of us may fall sick and even die. (1 Corinthians 11: 27-30)

All of us stand accused; guilty before God. So how can we live everyday knowing that we sin? What do we do once we have sinned? What do we do knowing that we had that wrong thought? What do we do knowing that we gave in to temptation--that our anger this week took over and got the best of us--that we did something to cause somebody to be mad at us--that we did something wicked against somebody because they hurt us--that we have sinned and are capable of sinning? How can we stand before God guilty and yet not be condemned?

Understanding Accusations

Chapter eight describes a woman who is dragged in the presence of Jesus for committing adultery. This woman stands accused. She says nothing. She stands before Christ knowing that she has committing adultery. There is a group of people that condemn her and totally embarrass this woman. How would you like to come before a crowd of people in the temple courts or in the church; stand in front of them, and be accused of your sin? How would you feel if your sin is broadcast in front of everyone? It says they brought her in the midst. They worked their way through the crowd, stood her in front of the crowd, and accused her. She was accused--how could she not be condemned?

If we analyze the accusation and the response of Jesus, we will understand why she was not condemned. If we look closely, the people who were accusing her were taking the truth and making it a lie. The Pharisees actually wanted to find a reason to drag Jesus and bring Him before the Sanhedrin and cause Him to be accused, convicted, and condemned. They desperately wanted to get Him. Nicodemus says, "Hey, hold on. Our law does not allow us to do that. You can't go get Him and judge Him and accuse Him without hearing from Him" (John 7:51). Because they were trying to tell Jesus how to function according to the law, they accused this woman, and even though they were right about it; they were turning the truth into a lie.

If we can understand the background to these events, we will be able to understand the process attached to it. In Old Testament times, if a person committed adultery, there had to be two witnesses to the sin being committed. They could not assume it happened because somebody came out of the door. They could not assume that something happened because they went on a date and they were not supposed to go on a date. After establishing the fact of adultery, the accusers had to bring the individuals before the judge. The judge would then condemn them both and not just the woman. (Deuteronomy 22:22) Both of them were to be convicted.

But what do this woman's accusers do? The Sanhedrin (which was composed of the High Priest, Sadducees, Pharisees and the Scribes) wanted to convict and condemn Jesus. It was not their motivation to set the wrong right; rather, they wanted to use this woman's sin to capture Jesus. If Jesus had said, "Stone her," He would have violated the Roman law by taking authority in His hands. If He had said, "Don't stone her," the teachers would have claimed that He had violated the law established by God. So either way, Jesus was trapped.

Here's what I want you to understand. Anytime you are being accused, it has to be for something that is a fact. When Satan goes to God and says, "God, your child did this or that," God looks down and makes sure that Satan is not lying. At any given time, if you are accused of something you did not commit, you are accused along with Christ.

1 Peter 3:13 says, "And who is there to harm you if you prove zealous for what is good?" When you are accused and you have not sinned, Christ stands accused with you. But when you sin, understand that you do stand accused. Why does Christ stand accused with us when we are falsely accused? It is because His Word is being tested!

The power of trying to live a holy life is that God can never be wrong. If you live a holy life before God and Satan goes up to heaven and says, "He has done this," just like he did with Job, God says, "You will check him out." What's God saying? I'm just as accused as my child is. That's the glory of walking holy.

It is better to be accused falsely than it is to sin. 1 Peter 3:17 says, "For it is better, if God should will it so, that you suffer for doing what is right rather than for doing what is wrong." When you are accused falsely, God fights the one who accuses you. Do right even when they falsely accuse you, boss you, and slander you, than sin against God. Be strong, you have the power of God with you.

When We Sin

There are consequences to sin. Folks keep putting their hands in the fire and want to know--how did I get pregnant? Why did I get this disease? Why are things going wrong with me? If you put your hands in the fire, they will get burnt. So the question is: what should you do when you sin?

The woman committed a sin. However, the reason why this woman continues to stand accused is because she does not understand that she is standing before Someone who can fix every sin in her life. Hence, she remains quiet. Read this carefully, I am going to share an awesome truth with you. When you do sin; if you confess your sin; He is faithful and just to forgive your sin. (1 John 1:9) Just go to God right away, confess your sin, He is faithful and just to forgive you. Satan brings it before Him, and God says, "I have forgiven them." Satan loses. That's why I am quick to say, "God, forgive me of my sins, cleanse me from all unrighteousness. God, I have done wrong, forgive me." When Satan stands up, he says, "Ha!" God says, "No, no, my word says this is done with. So, now what are you trying to tell me?"

The woman did not offer any defense. It is because she is looking for traditional means to confess her sin. She has committed adultery and she is expecting to be stoned to death and she says nothing. What do many people do? Do they say, "I need to call my pastor and tell him, so that he can go before God?" Wrong! They say, "I need to call my friends and tell them all about it, so that I can feel better." We're looking for traditional ways to deal with sin. Christ is saying,

"Listen, I died on the cross to remove your sin. Why are you sweating? Come to me!"

There's one thing I know about my son; when he's broke he knows how to call home. You don't have to call him and ask, "Do you need money?" He calls home and pride doesn't stop him from calling. Pride can prevent us from going before God and it will hurt us. We say, "Well, everybody sins. I am not the only one." Some of us like to look at preachers and find excuses. "See that Preacher, ha! He was not doing any good, so I did not even try. You see that Elder. You see that Deacon. You see that Minister." We'll end up bringing the "sinners" on a U-haul truck and line them up, but Christ will say, "I see you."

There's something negative about pride. What pride tends to do is cause God to fight you. So not only do you have a sin that is causing Him to look at you in a different way; now your pride causes Him to fight you. Why not just humbly come to Him and say, "God, I goofed, I messed up. When you died on the cross, you took care of my sins. Thank you, God."

The woman's guilt also caused her to keep quiet. Sometimes our guilt causes us not to have a defense. There are too many of us walking around guilty, saying, "I just don't know why I sinned. I can't really give my life to Christ. I am a bad person. You just don't know the things I did." Guilt causes us to stand accused and remain accused.

My sons talked me into getting another dog. This little puppy messed around in my house; a big no, no. When the puppy messed up, he had his head down, tail down, and just kept coming to me. He was looking at me, saying, "I am so guilty, I cannot look you in the

Guilty, but not Condemned **55**

eye. I cannot stand in front of you, so I'd rather walk by you and go outside and stay condemned." Don't let guilt make you stay away from church; stop you from fellowshipping with people; and stop you from talking to God. Christ says, "I know that you are guilty. I stayed on the cross for your sins. Your sins are as far as the east is from the west, so why are you carrying the load that does not belong to you?" Don't let guilt cause you to stand accused. Don't let it stand in the way of you being redeemed.

There is one more aspect that I would like to bring to your attention. If I were to put dirty clothes in the washing machine, wash them without using any detergent, they would still be pretty dirty. Since there was no detergent to pull the dirt out, when you put the clothes on; they will smell like you jogged yesterday.

Christ is saying that some of us come before Him, but we don't like the detergent. We are not willing to change. We say, "God, I am guilty, I have sinned, and I have done wrong, so help me, Lord." We then go right back out to the same nightclub, same party, same woman, same man, and the same sins. He's saying, "Hold on, I want to redeem you. I want the laundry detergent to go into the washer. It may bump you around, knock you from side to side, cause you to change, have you to think differently, operate differently, but that's what my blood does. It redeems! It restores and makes new creations." You need the blood of Christ to wash you. That's the thing I love about David. Did David sin? Yes, he did, and he said, "God, I have sinned, I am sorry." God responded, "David, there are consequences to sin." David then said, "Fix me, God." Then he was fixed and returned to his kingdom as a king. God forgave him.

Christ is Your Advocate

Christ does not let the woman fight for herself. Did you ever think--where is her mother? Where is her dad? Where is her husband? Where are her children, if she had any? Where is her family? What is so awesome is that Christ never leaves her. Those who want to stone her walk away when Christ challenges the sinless to throw the first stone (John 8:7).

The crowd is gone, but Christ never leaves her. Who speaks for her? Christ. She does not say anything; she is accused. Her guilt caused her to stay quiet. Tradition caused her to look to the priest and not Jesus. The great news is Christ speaks for her. When Satan goes to heaven and talks about you, then Christ speaks for you. He is your Advocate (1 John 2:1-2).

Read this passage and it will help you to take the necessary steps to faith when you stand accused. He never leaves you even when you stand accused. The Bible says that we are sealed for the day of redemption. Meaning, we are saved for eternity. Why do we sin now? This is because we work out our salvation with fear and trembling. (Philippians 2:12) When we are presenting our bodies as a living sacrifice, when we are dealing with our sins and growing spiritually, we cannot lose our salvation. We are sealed for the day of redemption; the day when rapture occurs.

Nothing will separate you from the love of God. No one can snatch you from His hands. He will hold you until He presents you before God. You are sealed! So stay there humbly before God and He will speak for you.

When Others Sin

No single person should stand alone, despite the sins they may have committed. The church should not walk away from sinners. That is considered a sin. That is being judgmental. God does not want us to judge others with the aim to point fingers at them. Too many people stand alone; and that's why Satan can tear them apart. When sin is dealt with incorrectly, it does not redeem people from their sin. In Matthew 18, when somebody messes up they don't have to fix it all before they come back. They come back and find a loving group of people who work with them so they can be fully restored.

Christ said, "I did not come to call the righteous, but sinners." (Matthew 9:13) The so-called perfect people did not care to hear Christ speak. The perfect people were the ones who nailed Him to a cross. Church is not for perfect people; it is for broken people who are willing to be made perfect. It is a spiritual hospital. Don't ever get the mindset that you have to be perfect to go to the house of the Lord. You will defeat the purpose of your life if you condemn and move away from those who may have committed a sin. You also need to remember to take out the plank from your own eye, before you start the process of restoring another person. A plank is pretty big; so don't get self-righteous. Deal with the plank in your own eye.

Matthew 18:15-16 says, "And if your brother sins, go and reprove him in private; if he listens to you, you have won your brother. But if he does not listen to you, take one or two more with you, so that by the mouth of two or three witnesses every fact may be confirmed."

You need to know for a fact that your brother sinned. It cannot be suspicion, presumption, or pre-supposition.

In Galatians 6:1, "Brethren, even if a man is caught in any trespass, you who are spiritual, restore such a one in a spirit of gentleness; each one looking to yourself, lest you too be tempted." The church is expected to deal with the sin, but God expects us to restore a person with gentleness. This is the process that God has created to help us from living in sin.

While helping others to deal with their sin, you should remember not to fall in the same trap yourself, "Lest you too may be tempted." There was a guy that confessed to a group of us guys that he was into pornography and he said, "I need some help."

He brought all the magazines and put them in front of us. We dealt with this whole thing. We listened, talked to him, and walked him through the system, which would hold him accountable. We hugged him, loved him, and told him that we will work through this with him.

Afterwards, we noticed all the magazines were sitting on the desk. We looked at each other, asking who is going to take them out. I asked the man to take them out, because when we are dealing with a sin, we have to be careful that we don't get caught in the very sin we are trying to help somebody deal with. If you are trying to stop individuals from going to a bar, or if they are already at a bar, let them come to you to work on that issue. Do not go to the bar and drink with them.

Two sins don't make a right. We need to correct the sin by working through it. We don't need to sin to make sure that the person does not stand alone.

When You Stand Accused

Remain with Jesus until He responds. The woman stayed. Look at all that's going on around her. They persist. The crowd says, "Come on, Christ, what are you going to do?" Christ is simply writing on the ground. Why was Christ writing on the ground? Why was He using His finger? If you look at the Old Testament, God gave the laws to Moses inscribed on tablets. (Exodus 32:16) Belshazzar's feast came to an end with the inscription on the wall. (Daniel 5) Christ is saying, "You are speaking to the Legislator about the law. I am in charge. I am not just your Teacher; I am the Law."

The woman saw Jesus Christ stooping, but she did not run. She could have been full of anxiety wondering what He was going to do, but she stayed. Jesus did not say anything immediately, but she stayed. Some of us go before God and ask for forgiveness. God doesn't reply according to our timelines and we take off. We should stay until you know He has responded. They that wait upon the Lord shall renew their strength and they will mount up like an eagle and soar. (Isaiah 40:31) Stay. Just wait. I know it is not the American way, but stay!

The woman did not run away. She did not talk and neither did she get arrogant. She did not say, "Well, if you only knew who was with me. I can quote Scripture too, you know, that the man is supposed to come with me. He's not here. Jesus, do you want to know who the man is? Why don't you fix him, Jesus? Do you know my husband is also fooling around? That's why I fool around." She didn't say anything. She just dealt with the fact that she was guilty and she stayed.

John says, "But when they persisted in asking Him, He straightened up, and said to them, 'He who is without sin among you, let him be the first to throw a stone at her' " (John 8:7). When Jesus was teaching the people, how was He teaching them? He was teaching them sitting down. When they asked Him a question about the law, what does He do? He bent down to respond to the question. When He decides to respond to the law, He looks in the eye. The woman stayed with Jesus and allowed Him to fight for her. And the result—all her accusers left, one by one. Too many of us run, but in the process we miss the total redeeming power of Christ.

Acknowledge what He has done. We must recognize what He has done or is doing before we can ever experience forgiveness. If you're still guilty today, it is because you are not cognitively acknowledging what He has done. Jesus asked the woman where her accusers were (John 8:10) as if He did not know similar to God asking, "Adam, where are you?" (Genesis 3:9). He asked her, "Did no one condemn you?" Now dwell on the woman's response: "No one, Lord." (John 8:11a)

This is the first and only place where this woman's words are recorded in the Bible and what did she say? *Lord!* She called Jesus, Lord, and at that very moment when she acknowledged what He had done for her, I believe she experienced His saving grace and love. John tells us: "And Jesus said, 'Neither do I condemn you; go your way. From now on sin no more.'" (John 8:11b)

Oh, how sweet are those words to a sinner—guilty, but not condemned! Remember Jesus Christ has to first get us to recognize what He is doing before we can truly experience forgiveness. The beauty of forgiveness is that it results in peace, joy, a cleared conscience, and a meaningful relationship with God.

Grace should stimulate us to be holy. Romans 6:1 says, "What shall we say then? Are we to continue in sin that grace might increase?" May it never be! Grace does not abound so we can sin. Rather, it should stimulate us to be holy. Grace abounds so that we have the room, the playing field, to grow spiritually. So that we can come to God when we sin and say, "God, forgive me," rather than having to seek salvation again. We just come to God and say, "God, forgive me, I am sorry, I have done wrong, and now God please remove that guilt from me." God says, "You stand forgiven. I have provided you grace, so you can mature to holiness."

1 John 3:6 reads as follows: "No one who abides in Him sins; no one who sins has seen Him or knows Him." All of us sin. It does not mean that we do not know Him. He is talking about a person who knowingly indulges in sin. That individual is never convicted, never feels bad, never tries to change, but just keeps committing sins. That person is still unsaved and that person does not know the Lord.

If you know Jesus Christ, you are a brand new creation. You don't keep hurting others—physically or emotionally, lying and cheating, and maliciously gossiping, and indulging in one sin after another without any deep conviction. If you lie, cheat, steal, fool around, and have no conviction with no desire to change, you are not saved. Get saved today, because He came to save you and He came to forgive you. Sin no more, Jesus told the woman and that is exactly what

He is telling you and me. Let us make an effort and let grace stimulate us to be holy.

In Conclusion

My son and I had a long talk and he said, "Dad, I don't know if I want to be a medical doctor, but I don't want to disappoint you." I said, "What gave you that idea?" He said, "Because you get excited when we talk about it." I said, "I get excited when you say you want to be a football player. No, son, I just want you to finish school and be productive. If you want to be a businessman, be the best businessman that you can be. Be godly and live a productive life. And I will sacrifice anything to help you along the way."

God is not demanding that you should become perfect. All He wants you to do is to commit to the process of growing to perfection. If you are not, become an active part of a body, because the church is His body. Learn from the Bible. Be committed to go out and do what God teaches you. Process! When you've sinned, you go before Him. When you have needs; pray. When you have burdens, tell Him. Be committed to the process. You don't have to be perfect to talk to Christ. You just need to be humble enough to accept your imperfections when you go before Christ.

In John 3:17: "For God did not send the Son into the world to judge the world, but that the world should be saved through Him." He did not come to condemn; He came to save. He did not come to wear you down; He came to restore your life. You need to focus on experiencing the joy of your salvation, rather than fearing constantly that God is coming to get you. Abide in His Word, learn from Him, trust in Him, depend on Him, call on Him, and have a relationship with Him that is free and total, intimate and personal. You go for it.

Yes, you are going to sin, make mistakes, and do some things that are not right. That does not mean that you should run away from God. Recently, I missed one of my son's games and I decided to go for his practice session. As I sat and watched my son practice, I said to myself, "My son plays really well!" The longer he is playing the better he is getting, because he is learning the system; learning how it works.

Christ says, "Walk with me and learn from me, so I can help you through every step of the way." Your sins need not destroy you. Rather, they should help you understand the offense better and to practice your defense harder. Remember: The only way you can experience God and have power over sin is by staying with Jesus and acknowledging your sin and accepting the Lord's saving grace today.

If you are beaten down by sin, stay at the cross. Christ has the power to fix your life. Let Him fix it. Delve in His Word. Accept your mistakes. Don't let pride and traditions get in the way. Just deal with your sin, because if you confess, He is faithful. He will listen to you and forgive you. It is a done deal!

Take your steps to faith and allow Him to cleanse you today. Don't let sin drive you into the ground. Instead, let His grace build you up and help you soar in the sky.

CHAPTER 5

Loving the Unlovable

And He said to him, "'You shall love the Lord your God with all your heart, and with all your soul, and with all your mind.' This is the great and foremost commandment. The second is like it, 'You shall love your neighbor as yourself.' On these two commandments depend the whole Law and the Prophets." (Matthew 22:37-40)

I want you to visualize someone in your life--whether it is a fellow employee or an employer, a husband or a wife, a family member or an irritating relative--someone that just drives you crazy. It could be your ex-husband or your ex-wife. It could be your spouse's ex-husband or wife. It may even be someone from another race. You wish you did not have to see this person that they would leave you alone and that they were never born. To make matters worse, they seem to be more blessed than you are. In fact, they seem to be the ones with the bigger home, nicer friends, and a better life, while you are struggling along.

As you picture that unlovable person around you, I want to prepare you to take some important steps to faith, because I do not believe that that person is accidentally around you. If you were to go to a different job, they may come in a different dress or a different suit, but they will show up again. You may decide to move and that neighbor may turn out to be worse than the one from whom you were running. I don't believe God allows that person to arrive at your address by accident. You may actually leave your spouse for a better life, only to find you have jumped from the frying pan to the fire. In short, running away is not the answer when God is challenging you to learn to love the unlovable.

A Deeper Understanding

The world says hate those who are trying to hurt you. Interestingly, that is exactly what the Jewish leaders taught their followers when Jesus walked on this earth. Leviticus 19:18 explicitly says, "You shall not take vengeance, not bear any grudge against the sons of your people, but you shall love your neighbor as yourself; I am the Lord."

However, the Pharisees added to the law by saying, "You must be faithful to God and believe in God and oppose those who oppose God. Therefore, you must hate those who do not support God, who are stopping us from worshipping God, who are coming against us and taking the money that belongs to God and taxing us for Caesar."

The Jews hated the Jewish tax collectors who were going against the Jewish beliefs and taxing their own people by working for a foreign government that was oppressing them. They also hated the pagans, including the Samaritans, who lived between Judea and Galilee.

Well, times have changed--or have they? You may be thinking that you do not hate Jewish tax collectors

Loving the Unlovable **66**

or Samaritans but I want to urge you to look deep within yourself. Many of us believe that we should hate the Muslims, hate those who perform abortions, hate the homosexuals. We like to shake our heads and say, "Look at what they are doing. They are killing babies. Look at their lifestyle. They oppose God and do not support God." We may not like to use the word hate and even try to avoid using it, but the strong feelings that we have can very well be described as hatred.

The word "hate" means to have a particular wish that some evil would come upon someone. The moment a homosexual gets AIDS, we say, "They deserved it." The Bible says that is hate. The minute someone is punished by another race, we say, "They deserved it, look at what they did to us." The minute our employer dies or comes up with cancer, we say, "They were mean and rude and God is just paying them back." If our best friend went against us and then really goes through a hard time, we say, "They deserved it."

The Bible explicitly states that the two greatest commandments not only involve loving God with all our heart, soul, and mind, but also loving our neighbor as our self. In fact, on these two commandments depend the whole law and the prophets (Matthew 22:37-40).

Jesus wants us to understand that our love for God is demonstrated by our love for our neighbor, that is, those who come in contact with us. If you really love God, His commandments, and His Word, your love for God is going to move you to love those around you. His Word never moves us to love ourselves and become selfish. It is not surprising that the Bible emphasizes that those who claim to love God but hate their neighbor do not really know God (1 John 4:20).

An intimate relationship with God results in love for others. Some individuals like to say that they love God and yet hate their mate. It's like saying you want to jump in the swimming pool without getting wet. Indeed, if you want to know the depth of a person's walk with God, watch how that person treats other people.

You may be saying, "I don't want to mistreat anyone." How do we function when people are downright unlovable? Some people are just mean. Some people are not happy until things are messy. Some will go out of their way to make things difficult for you. Some will give you a cold shoulder through no fault of your own and throw false accusations at you.

It is difficult when our friends, families, and co-workers encourage us to dislike somebody who is obnoxious. It is difficult when our background influences us to ignore people that bug us. It is difficult when our feelings tell us to get back against those individuals who use us to get what they want. It is difficult, at that time, to love the unlovable because our emotions tell us to fight them and to do what it takes so that they can feel the pain that they inflicted on us. Our emotions are so powerful that they can totally dominate us and make us question--God, how do you expect me to love somebody who is unlovable?

Commit to Obey Christ

Yes, God does expect us to love the unlovable. Love in the Bible is not described as a feeling. So stop concentrating on how you feel about that person or issue or what someone did to you, look to Jesus and commit to do what God calls you to do with that person. I do want to clarify something at this point. God is not commanding you to like somebody. You may not like the way someone behaves, but you can still love that person.

The issue in the Bible is taking care of the first commandment. Are you going to love the Lord with all your heart, your soul, and your mind? The minute you decide to love Him, He says, "I will transform you to love the unlovable." We have to make the decision to preserve His commandments by following the law of Christ, not the law of man. The law of man demands that you fight back. The law of man encourages you to hurt those who hurt you. The law of Christ wants you to turn your other cheek. (Matthew 5:39) It is a different law. It is a different word. It is a different way of operating in Christ.

You say, "But God, you said in the Scriptures that we should hate our mother and father, brothers and sisters in order to follow you." (Luke 14:26) He says, "I want you to give me priority. But I do not want you to have a malicious desire to wish evil upon someone." (Matthew 10:37)

You say, "God, what about the homosexuals? They commit a despicable sin. Homosexuality is an abomination to you. Why do you expect me to love them, God? We ought to hate them and nail them to a tree." God says, "No, hate their sin, but not them."

"But God, look at all these babies that are being aborted, thousands of them just in the black clinic alone. What about blowing up the clinic; shooting the doctor?" God says, "Not at all, hate the sin, but not the people."

I never ask my sons if they *feel* like taking out the trash, *feel* like cleaning their room, *feel* like taking a shower, *feel* like going and washing the car, *feel* like mowing the yard; the feeling is irrelevant.

My son told me the other day, "Dad, I don't feel like washing the puppy and cleaning up the backyard and doing all this stuff with the dog."

I said, "Son, I told you if you don't want the consequences, don't get the dog. She is your dog. You named her. Now take care of her."

That is why the Bible says, "Love your enemy." It has nothing to do with feelings; rather, it has everything to do with your commitment to obey God. When you choose to obey God, the love of God is perfected in you (1 John 2:5).

Allow me to share a story with you. In the midst of a battle, when bullets were flying everywhere, a man in a foxhole realized that his comrade in the other foxhole was badly hurt. The injured soldier in the second hole had always given the man in the first hole a hard time.

Although, it seemed tempting to leave the injured soldier in his hole and allow him to die, the first man decided that turning away from his injured soldier was not an option for him. He crawled on his stomach, barely missing the bullets that were being shot around him and jumped into the hurt comrade's foxhole and helped him to survive. He put aside his emotions and risked his life to help his comrade according to the law of the army.

Well, the above narration poses an important question to us. When our emotions are strong and we are being fired at, are we going to listen to our feelings or are we going to have a deep commitment and choose to obey Christ?

It is my prayer that we will choose to obey Christ.

Role of the Tongue

Does it surprise you that you can come to church and say, "Praise the Lord, Thank you, Jesus, " with your tongue, and then somebody steps on your toe and you use the same tongue to use harsh, destructive words? Same tongue—it is like a deadly poison. It is a restless evil (James 3:8).

That's why folks can leave church, go home, and talk to their children, husband and wife as mean as ever, even though they just got through singing to Jesus. Out of this tongue comes cursing and praising (James 3:9). Make every effort to control your tongue (Proverbs 10:19) and do not use filthy language (Ephesians 4:29).

That's why God gave us teeth and lips in front of it. He also gave us two hands because we sometimes have to put our hands over our mouth in order to have our lips obey our tongue. If we are able to control our tongue, we will be able to follow the law of Christ by loving the unlovable.

Operating like Jesus

My son walked in the room one day and said, "I am just like you. I even think like you." Because my son spends time around me, he has started to act like me. God made us in His image (Genesis 1:27), and then He told us to multiply (Genesis 1:28). What is He trying to say? He is saying, "You're supposed to be just like your parents, but your parents are supposed to have my image." When we learn to operate like Jesus, we will naturally learn to love like Jesus.

Christ is saying, "If you respond to my discipline--because I discipline those I love (Hebrews 12:7). If you respond to my Word, I guarantee that you will have the same mind and the same attitude that I have. You will be like me. When people were mocking me, when they were laughing at me, when they put nails in my hands and a crown of thorns on my head. When they slit a hole in my side, I said, 'Father, forgive them for they know not what they are doing.'" (Luke 23:34)

Yes, Christ said in the Garden of Gethsemane, "Father, let this cup pass from me." (Matthew 26:39) His emotions were strong, but Christ chose to fulfill the will of God. (Matthew 26:42) He chose to love the unlovable, those people who were despicably against Him, and thus completed His Father's business.

Vengeance Belongs to the Lord

You were not created to take vengeance. Hatred leads to anger and bitterness, which can result in a vengeful spirit. When you decide to take a wrong course of action, you must know that you will have to deal with the consequences. I always tell my kids, "Please know this and know this well. If you go out there and you get into trouble and you commit a crime, your dad is going to help you spend time in the prison, because I know your mother and I trained you right." My son said, "Dad, what if it is a life sentence." I said,

"I will come to see you; I will pray with you; I will hold your hand, but you are going to stay there. You better be glad it is a life sentence and not a death sentence. But you must know the consequences; and if you're not willing to deal with the consequences, don't get involved in the act."

Some people like to say, "Oops, I got involved in an affair." That is a serious matter, it can destroy families. An affair is not an "oops" matter. If you don't want the consequences, don't get involved in the action. There was a young lady who was killed during the Gulf War and her parents said, "Oh, we cannot believe that she is dead. She only joined the army as a weekend soldier for the money. She did not really mean to go and fight in a war." That was an extremely sad situation, but I thought to myself--she knew that she had joined the army. She knew they could call her if there was a war. If she did not want to fight in a war, she should have found some other part-time job. Don't join the army and then not expect them to call you to war.

God says, "Vengeance is mine." (Deuteronomy 32:35, Hebrews 10:30) If we don't want the consequences, don't violate the law of Christ. Let Him deal with those who have wronged you and you will not have regrets in life.

Love in Action

A man was getting ready to jump from the plane and parachute down to the ground when he realized that the guy ahead of him was having trouble with his parachute. The pilot told the first man, "You must jump and help him." The first man replied, "Not at all. That's the risk he was willing to take when he decided to jump." "All you have to do is get your head straight and you will catch up with him, because his parachute is still fluttering, and therefore, slowing him down. Just jump" advised the pilot. "Nope!" said the man: "I don't even know the guy. Why should I jump?"

The man eventually decided to jump and help the guy in distress. Both of them landed safely. The first man stated grouchily, "Man, I did not enjoy helping you." The other guy replied, "Even though you did not want to help me, you did help me. I appreciate it anyway." Love is, my friend, an act.

You may say you love everyone, including the unlovable. If your words are not supported by actions, then you need to check your heart. Love will always lead to positive actions.

Praying for Your Enemy

Do you know that God tells us to pray for our enemies to help us to overcome our hatred? The moment it is said, "Let us pray for our enemy," people respond, "I can't do that!" Most people automatically think that they need to ask God to bless their enemy. That is not necessarily true.

Let me give you an illustration. When we were in our Center, the owner gave us a very hard time, "You all left trash in the backyard." We responded, "Sir, we have not been in the backyard. There are no cars pulled up there." The owner then says, "Well, it is your trash." "Does it have our name on it? "It is your trash. Pick it up." We just agreed, "Yes, sir."

I said, "But the air conditioning is not working right." Owner says, "Well, if I fix it, I'm raising the rent. And if you don't accept my terms, I am going to

Loving the Unlovable **74**

kick you out." I dealt with that week after week, day after day. Sometimes he would come by drunk and start screaming. "You have not paid the rent?" "I did." "I don't see it on my desk." "It is there." "You are a month behind. I am going to throw you out."

When I was locking the doors for the last time, some emotions popped up in me. I really wanted to pray, but the question in my mind was, "How am I going to pray? God, kill him. Send the moon down right on top of his truck while he's driving." I could not do that, because I know that God wants me to love and pray. How could I pray for him and love him at the same time?

Habakkuk was mad at the Babylonians. You ever read Habakkuk's prayer? He was mad at the Babylonians for coming and ripping apart God's people, and he prayed to God. "Your eyes are too pure to approve evil, And You cannot look on wickedness with favor. Why do You look with favor on those who deal treacherously? Why are You silent when the wicked swallow up, those more righteous than they?" (Habakkuk 1:13)

As long as you and I stay in the Word and not violate His Word, and pray, we are praying for our enemy. You don't have to pray, "God, bless them; keep them; let their family be blessed; let all the money in the world fall down upon them so they be rich and productive and live a beautiful life."

When David's enemy was against him, what did David pray? "I will extol You, O Lord, for You have lifted me up, And have not let my enemies rejoice over me." (Psalm 30:1) What did Moses say? "God, these are your people. You can't let your people die out here because you would look bad." (Exodus 32:11-12)

So I prayed, "Lord, this man gave your people a hard time. Let him know that he cannot touch your people and keep on moving. He must know that you are alive. He must know that you mean business. But God, I don't want you to hurt him. I don't want his body to rot with diseases, and I do not want to hate him." Did I pray for my enemy? Yes. Now, he must face God. And what am I going to do now? I planning on driving over there and saying once more, "Do you want to talk about God now?"

The Bible says, "Pray for your enemies" (John 5:45). As long as you stay in the Word, you should pray, and not with vengeance. Pray so that your enemies will know that God is God. You don't have to pray "sweet nothings" all the time. You must stay in the Word and not hate.

When Jesus was put on the cross, He prayed for those who persecuted Him. He knew that God's wrath is going to fall on those who know no remorse, and He prayed for forgiveness. When Peter cut off the servant's ear, Christ put it back on. You live by the sword; you die by the sword (Matthew 26:52). Christ actually does what He is telling us to do. That's why folks, we must follow Christ and not the world.

A Believer's Role

Very often we like to be with people who share our color, education, viewpoints, neighborhood, and lifestyle. Christ says in Matthew 5:46, "For if you love those who love you, what reward have you? Do not even the tax-gatherers do the same?"

As the senior pastor of my church, I am never happy watching a group of people always staying in their comfort zone. When we do that, we automatically determine that we will not grow. If you are not willing to move away from your comfort zone, you will stagnate.

I see this in high schools all the time--varsity players hang out with varsity players. I even heard that a junior varsity player walked into the senior varsity players' locker room once and they beat him up and threw him out. "Boy, you don't come in here. You got to earn the right to be here." Cliquish—that's what we are; we find our zones and we like to stay there.

What should be a believer's role? "And let us consider how to stimulate one another to love and good deeds." (Hebrews 10:24) "That person looks kind of down. She's a single parent and it looks like she's got a lot of load on her. I am going to consider how I can go over there and help her. This happened today with Lisa. John has a need. I am going to consider how I can help out."

That's what church is about. That is the role of a disciple of Christ. If someone does not feel like shaking hands and hugging, you still hug them and shake their hands. Can you imagine what would happen if we would stimulate one another every Sunday morning? Imagine how many people would leave encouraged because the gift of love is present.

In the New Testament, you see people fellowshipping because they were considering how to stimulate other people to love and good deeds. Indeed, when you move outside your comfort zone, it becomes profitable for the church, and therefore, for you. Do not come to church, hear a sermon, read some Scripture, and go home. Come to church because you have a job to do and that involves moving outside your comfort zone and sharing the love of Jesus.

Ask questions.

Show concern.

Share burdens.

"How was your day? What's going on in your life? How is your family doing?" Some may say that is being nosy. Well, what God thinks is what matters most. Do you love others in obedience to God? If the answer is yes, then keep up the good work.

I do understand that loving the unlovable is not an easy task. We have to manage our emotions, control our tongue, capture our thoughts, manage our prayer life, and trust God when all the time it seems like the other person is winning. This is especially hard when our flesh is at work against the Spirit and the Spirit against the flesh. These two elements of our lives are constantly at work. (Galatians 5:16-18) Paul instructed young pastor Timothy to watch out for himself (1 Timothy 4:16) and the elders of Ephesus to do the same. (Acts 20:28)

Our greatest enemy is actually not the person, but what that person exposes about us. God is actually doing us a favor by allowing us to concentrate on His call to discipleship, which is to deny ourselves (Luke 14:26) and put to death the flesh (Colossians 3:9-10) while He fights our enemy.

I always encourage believers to be totally honest with God when they have to deal with the unlovable. Again, I do not ask you to foster hatred, but tell God all about your struggles and difficulties that an unlovable person or persons may be causing you.

Secondly, it helps to share your feelings with a trusted friend, so others can pray for you. You must remember to walk in the Spirit by maintaining your focus on your spiritual growth. It's like driving in bad weather. Everyone wants to obey all the traffic laws because of the unpredictable nature of the environment. We are not trying to fight other drivers; rather, we are simply trying to protect ourselves.

Finally, God has provided the church as protection to believers. We must remain faithful to the church and in the midst of loving the unlovable take time to love those who love us and we will find strength. It is never good to isolate yourself when dealing with the unlovable. In fact, it is necessary that we surround ourselves with people who care for us. More importantly, when you are threatened by the unlovable, try never to be alone with the person, because while you are always encouraged to love, you are never expected to be foolish.

Do everything you can to maintain the peace of God in your life. This is done by capturing thoughts and praying when anxious (Philippians 4:4-7) about everything in your life. Dwell on things that are true, honorable, right, pure, lovely, and of good repute (Philippians 4:8-9). Hatred leads to bitterness, which leads to destruction, but love leads to life and joy. Always remember the best way to control a bad situation is to believe that God is indeed in control.

Loving the Unlovable **79**

When you Love the Unlovable

Growth takes place. When you make an effort to reach out to the unlovable, you start practicing the Word of God. If you are always hanging around with folks you like, you are not required to practice anything. Those folks are doing the things you want them to do; therefore, your actions do not result in growth.

"But solid food is for the mature, who because of practice (because they put it to work) have their senses trained to discern good and evil" (Hebrews 5:14). What is the author saying? The person who hears the Word, but does not do anything, miscalculates. Growth comes from practice, not from staying in the same clique, but by reaching out and loving the unlovable.

Intimacy develops. When you try to love the unlovable, you develop an intimacy with Christ. What a wonderful privilege. You get to know Christ. His love is perfected in you as you obey His Word and God considers you His friend.

Transformation occurs. Loving the unlovable transforms the world. Why do many people think that Christians are quite unlovable? We may go to church, but we leave our knowledge there and do not put what we learn to work. We hate like they hate; we despise people like they despise people. We don't want to interact with this kind of person or that kind of person and sometimes, any kind of person. A non-Christian does not see God alive in us. Do you think that Jesus said, "The world will know that you are my disciples by the way you come to church?" No! "The world will know that you are my disciples by the way you read the Word?" No! He says, "By this all men will know that you are my disciples, if you have love for one another" (John 13:35). Action--and that is why Jesus says, "This I command you, that you love one another" (John 15:17).

When we refuse to love the unlovable, we become good for nothing. Look at the church at Ephesus. Did they know the Word? Oh, yes! They could tell you the Word. They did not need any correction when the book of Ephesians was written. By the time Revelations was written, Christ was threatening to walk out of the door because they had left their first love. They had the Word; they could break it down, but they had lost their first love.

Matthew 5:13 says, "You are the salt of the earth; but if the salt has become tasteless, how can it be made salty again? It is no longer good for anything, except to be thrown out and trampled underfoot by men." You are the salt, but if you don't want to love, obey God, or focused on what God is calling you to do; then you will not be good for anything. You will not be good for your marriage, for your job, or for your church. Transformation occurs when you decide to love the unlovable. Surely, the world becomes a better place to live when you share the love of Christ.

God's name is glorified. "You are the light of the world. Let your light shine before men in such a way that they may see your good works, and glorify your Father who is in heaven" (Matthew 5:14-16). His name is glorified when we make a decision to love someone who may be struggling with drugs, alcohol, or prostitution. When we choose to love the unlovable, the name of God is glorified. When we refuse to follow the laws of the world and choose to follow the laws of

Loving the Unlovable **81**

Christ, we magnify the name of the Lord and thirsty souls are drawn near to Him.

God chose us in Him before the foundation of the world so that we should be holy and blameless before Him. (Ephesians 1:4) He called us to be holy. By obeying God's Word, we become holy. God says, "I called you so that people on earth would see me everyday and have a reason to trust me, obey me, lean on me, because they find you who know me to be blameless on account of me."

Why is it so hard for us to walk across and greet someone who may be going through a difficult time? Why is it so hard to extend a hand of friendship to someone in need? God allows rain to fall on the righteous and the unrighteous. He never stops loving the sinners, rather He wants them to come to Him and accept eternity. Indeed, "For God so loved the world, that He gave His only begotten Son, that whoever believes in Him should not perish, but have eternal life." (John 3:16)

If we quit loving the unlovable, the drunk will stay a drunk and the drug addict will stay a drug addict. That person, who does not know Jesus, will never come to Him. That single parent who is struggling will never experience the love of God, because we chose to shut the door on them and move in the direction that was most comfortable for us.

So many people continue to fall apart, because we prefer to point our fingers and say, "Look at them." Christ is saying, "Look at you. You are the salt of the earth. You are the light of the world. You are supposed to make a change. Don't look at them; they're in sin. They do not know the truth. But you know the truth and you are supposed to love. You are supposed to follow me." We cannot say that we love God and not love the unlovable.

Take yet another step to faith and make a decision to love the unlovable today.

CHAPTER 6

A Better Sacrifice

By faith Abel offered to God a better sacrifice than Cain, through which he obtained a testimony that he was righteous, God testifying about his gifts, and through faith, though he is dead, he still speaks. (Hebrews 11:4)

Is it faith when a solider joins the army? Is it faith when he really goes to war? Is it faith when students pick up their test books, notebooks, and backpacks to go to school? Is it faith when they apply themselves at school believing that having good grades will get them into college and allow them to be effective in the market place? Is it faith when a person goes to a doctor's office and gives all the information a doctor needs to make a diagnosis? Is it faith when that person actually purchases the medication prescribed and takes it? Also, is it faith when we say that Jesus died on Calvary's cross and that He rose from the dead or is it faith when we actually live our lives based on the gospel?

Belief or Faith?

When we stop at stating our beliefs, then that is exactly what it remains—our beliefs. A belief system means to believe enough in something so as to rest on it because it is factual and in your face. Faith is when you can't see what is going to happen, but you have the assurance that it will happen and you expect it to happen. Whether you see it or not, you expect it will get done. This is why the author of Hebrews states that faith gives us confidence. Yes, he is talking about confident expectation and unwavering conviction.

In other words, the Bible is pointing out that everyday of your life, you see things that once were not seen, but are now seen. You see a tree that was not a tree and when God spoke, it became a tree. Everyday we experience things that He says He is going to do. Those who state that they believe in their hearts that Jesus is going to do all that He has promised for His followers, yet do not have the assurance that God will do it, stand convicted. They are not really convinced that God is going to do what He says He is going to do.

This is why such people tell you all about Scripture and what you should do, but they don't do anything about it themselves. They don't really have the assurance or conviction that He will do what He says He is going to do. The Bible is saying there could be people that know Scripture and can comment on it. In fact, they know every theological system of the Bible; however, having information does not mean they have faith. Yes, it does mean that they have knowledge of God, a belief system, but it stops right there.

Knowledge without faith is limited. Knowledge that spurs you to faith will take you to higher ground. If a person believes that a plane will take him to his destination, he will jump into it. If a person believes that a medicine will work, she will take it. If a person believes that a car will function, he will drive it. Similarly, if people believe that Jesus will do for them according to the Word of God, they will act on it. Our faith should never be just about having a belief system; not only about saying that Jesus Christ came for everybody.

The Bible challenges us to have the kind of faith that is willing to share the love of Christ with every person. Even though you don't see the person change, get off drugs, a family doing great, or finances getting better, faith is the conviction that Jesus can make a difference. We want to share the gospel, become mentors, and effectively work with those whom God brings along our path because faith is a conviction. Even though I don't see what I am working towards, I am going to act like I see it. That is moving from belief to faith.

There are too many believers that have a belief system and no faith. We say we believe Jesus died on the cross, the Romans nailed Him there, and the Jews mocked Him while He was nailed there, because it says so in history books. This does not require faith; it is a belief, because it is recorded in history. Five hundred people saw Jesus after the resurrection; we technically don't have to have faith for this. In fact, Thomas touched His side and checked the holes in His hands.

We have to have faith if our wife is not acting right to love her unconditionally and when our husband is not acting right to submit to him. We have to have faith when it is time to share the gospel even though people are abusing us and saying all kinds of things about us. We have to have faith when our world is falling apart and our bodies are decaying and yet we stand convinced that Jesus is Lord of all. Indeed, the Bible tells us to love our enemies and when we do love them we move from a belief system to faith.

There is a story about a top Boeing engineer who was flying a propeller plane. This was right before the era of 707 jet planes that promised to travel the sky at high rates of speed and deliver people to their destinations a whole lot faster than a propeller plane. The guy sitting next to the engineer in the propeller plane asked the engineer what he thought about the 707 planes. The engineer started to describe how the jet moved and how it operated and about the role of the wind and the air. The first guy was duly impressed and said, "Man, you know a lot," and the engineer proudly responded by saying that he was the designer of the 707.

The other guy said, "Well, how come you are not flying in it." The engineer replied that he wanted it to be tested with others before he actually got in it. The guy stated, "You designed the plane and tell me how good it is with all the backup systems so even if one of the engines goes out the weight does not fall on one wing. You tell me about aerodynamics and computers that keep things going and how it monitors the levels of the plane so that the pilot can basically fly looking at the instrument panel. You are telling me these things yet you are not in the plane!" Let me tell you why the engineer was not in the plane. It is because the engineer had all the data, but he did not have faith.

Any person that decides to walk by faith has decided to act on the Word and not just hear it. Faith is not a lot of Bible knowledge, but what you do with the knowledge. It is one thing to be educated about parachutes, but it is another thing to actually jump out of the plane and use the parachute.

One time I fixed the brakes for my wife's car and she asked me if I did it right. I took pictures and everything else to make sure I had everything right. She asked me if I had tested the brakes and I said yes. Then she asked me to drive the car the next day, and only after it had worked for me all-day, she stated that she would be willing to drive it the following day. In other words, even though she had all the information, she did not believe me. She said since you believe the information, you act on it. The bottom line is she did not have faith.

A Worthy Offering

Amazingly, faith develops a dependency that makes it no longer about us, because it kills our worldly opinions and feelings and makes us totally dependent on God. This is especially difficult in our society, because we have to be that somebody that society wants us to be. If we have an education, we become valuable. If we have money or a nice car, we are counted important. If we live in the suburbs, then we are considered better. Jesus, however, has a totally different definition. He says if you are saved, you are slaves to righteousness. He doesn't call us to become successful; instead, He calls us to be dependent on Him.

The Bible tells us that, by faith, Abel offered to God a better sacrifice. Have you ever wondered why Abel's sacrifice was considered better than Cain's offerings? In Genesis 4, we find that one brother took care of animals while the other took care of the fields. God testifies saying that He really appreciated and respected Abel's offering better than He did Cain's.

God saw Abel's offering as better because Abel brought to God the firstborn of his flock.

Many of us know that people who breed dogs get the purest bred dogs to get the best bloodline. When they get the best bloodline, the value of the dogs goes up. It is not any different than when you are raising sheep, cows or chicken; you take the best of the best and you use it to get the best bloodline to get the highest price. Abel took the best and he gave that to God. Moreover, the verse goes on to say that he took the fatlings, meaning the fat of the animals, and he gave it to God.

We have to understand that there was no law during Abel's lifetime that said you must give this or give that. Indeed, there was no Mosaic Law that told him that he should give unto God. In fact, Abel did not have a Bible. Abel simply watched the glory of God and more than likely listened carefully to his parents as they described how God created the earth and is the One who sustains all things. We must know that Adam and his family continued to have a relationship with God--even though it is not the same as living in the Garden of Eden--so Abel is able to understand the concept of God. He is so appreciative of all that God has done that he not only brings the very best of the very best, he cuts out the fat and he offers that to the Lord with humbleness and gratefulness.

Abel understood that God is the very reason that he has what he has and he is giving God back the blessing that God gave him. Instead of depending on his own wisdom, Abel was willing to trust God to keep the flock at its best quality. Abel's willingness to give to God indicates that he was very much aware that the

A Better Sacrifice **89**

only reason he had flock and other blessings was because of the mercy of God.

Cain offered whatever he could find in the field. The Bible does not say he got the very first thing that he planted. He just picked up what was available from the field and brought it to God. Doesn't that sound like the dollar we bring to church saying that is the best we can do at this time because we have a lot of bills. Let me reiterate that it is not that Abel does not have a lot of bills, but Abel realized that the only reason he has a job in the first place is because of God.

The only reason I am able to drive to my apartment or house is because of God; the only reason there is a bus line in front of my home is because of God. Since He has proven himself to be God, Abel is saying, he would rather be convicted by the evidence that is in front of him to go ahead and give to God. He has the assurance that God will keep giving him evidence of His goodness. Indeed, Abel has the assurance that God will keep giving him blessings that will be more abundant and above all that he could ask or think. Since Able has this assurance, he was willing to give to God even though he was unable to see the blessings at that time. He was led to exercise faith, because the evidence that God is going to do what He says He will do convicted him.

Abel's offering was better because of his attitude, mindset, and the level of dependency he showed on God. He was saying, "God I so depend on you and trust you that you don't have to show me the blessing I will get tomorrow or even how you are going to take care of me next week." The evidence of God taking care of Abel at that time was enough for him to do what was best towards God.

There was a child in Guyana that got a dollar as his allowance. This child, after receiving his dollar, asked his daddy what his father wanted.

The father replied, "Son, it is your money, keep it."

The son said, "No daddy, what do you want."

The father trying to please his son asked for a lollipop. The kid bought the lollipop and brought it to his daddy and asked his father how much money he had left. His daddy told him that he had about seventy-five cents left.

The son insisted, "Daddy, that's a lot of money! What you asked for wasn't anything, what else do you want?"

The daddy stated, "Son, I gave you the money so you could have some."

The son's response brings us back to dependency. He stated, "Daddy, I have you, so what do you want me to bring for you now!"

This kid was willing to give his father the whole dollar, because he knew that since he belonged to his father, he would receive another dollar in the coming week. Even though he did not see his dollar for the following week, he was willing to trust the evidence and give up the dollar for the week.

God is saying that this is what made Abel's offering better. Abel knew that God was the one that made the animals. God just said let there be a dog, let there be a lion, let there be a bear, let there be a sheep, let there be a goat and there they were. So if God could make an animal out of nothing, why should I sweat about giving Him one animal today? Abel showed total dependency on God.

Dependency and Worship

Do you know that our dependency on God is a form of worship? When we don't act dependent on God, we are not focusing on his worthiness; rather, we are talking about our own worthiness. We are saying, "God I can't trust you so I am going to give you a dollar because we have to make it." God is saying we are giving more respect to what we are going to do than to what He can do. We are giving like Cain gave, but we cannot worship until we present our bodies as a living sacrifice. Until we decide that it is all about God and act accordingly, our lukewarm worship is not pleasing to God. Every time we sacrificially help someone in need we show our dependency on God. You are willing to give your offering because God has blessed you. You and I know that we would not be alive, but by the grace of God. When we are able to see the evidence of God's grace, it should cause us to have faith in showing grace to someone else and this is true worship that pleases God.

I know it is hard to give that offering and share with others when we feel like we barely have anything for ourselves. It is nerve wracking to give someone your last ten dollars knowing that it is your lunch money. I can never forget the days when the neighborhood kids would come over and my wife wanted to witness to this particular kid at a time when I had not been paid for two months. In order for the one kid to come, it meant that other kids had to come in with him. So here we were preparing our last meal for the whole neighborhood. It was unnerving to sit at the table and hear my wife saying, "Preacher, trust in God," and she was rubbing it in. I was sitting there going, "Yeah I trust Him, but all your little dudes need to go home." Oh, I know giving is not the most awesome feeling all the time, which is why He says our offering becomes a sacrifice that God sees as worship. It is not when we do what we want to do. It is when we go against the grain and share His blessings, He takes notice of our efforts and is pleased with us.

I have to be honest and say that I do not enjoy conversing with people every time I travel. This is my time of no phones, no appointments, this is my time to get out my laptop. Someone will bug me and I say, "God has to put me next to this person for a reason." It is not always pleasant, that's why it becomes a sacrifice. It is not something that fits our schedule; in fact, if you have children you will understand what I am talking about. Children never cry when you've had enough sleep. It's when you are broke that they have to go to the doctor. I have seen my son, sick as a dog, and by the time we get to the doctor's office he is running around eating candy. I am saying to myself, "Boy, you were sick when we left the house, why are you acting like nothing is wrong now." Kids have taught me to live sacrificially. Jesus is saying that when we move from normal to sacrificial, because of His Word, we take yet another step to faith.

Not surprisingly that the Scripture says that though Abel is dead, his gift still speaks. In fact, the Bible challenges us to look at Abel and Abraham, who had no law, but they gave, and God was pleased because they gave willingly and sacrificially. A person that does not give is a person that does not totally depend on God and hence, is not demonstrating faith. I don't care how much a person says, "I love the Lord! I cry for Him!" The Bible says your heart is where you hold your treasure. If you say you love God, you will make sure that the work of the Kingdom of God is getting done. If our funds are going to build our kingdom only, then it means we love ourselves and not God and we do not have a committed life.

A Greater Dependency

Speaking of dependency, we are told that by faith Enoch was taken up after he had lived 865 years (Hebrews 11:5). The brother didn't jog a day in his life or try to buy a bunch of herbs. I went to one of those places and the guy was explaining how herbs did all these things and I said, "Man, I am not a cow! Give me some bacon and eggs and I will jog it off." The guy said that causes higher cholesterol levels, so I told him I would eat it once a week. Enoch didn't have an exercise program at Bally's, but he certainly lived and walked with God. My friend, faith makes you so dependent that it determines the way you live everyday. Faith is so dependent on God that it controls our actions at work, in the grocery store, and while driving. In fact, God controls even our secret moments--when no one is looking--because we are committed to depending on Him.

One day a pastor asked me if I would come and preach on commitment and I told him that I wasn't going to waste his money, because this isn't something I can preach about. You can only grow people to be committed and this is why I believe in life application. People will go to the mall and if they cannot find that shoe, they want they will drive all the way across town to another mall. If someone gives us a job on the ship paying 90,000 dollars, we will take that job and stay committed to the boss. Yet, we find it hard to remain committed to Jesus and His Word.

Offering for Recognition

Jesus Christ exhorts us not to make an offering for the purpose of gaining recognition from mankind. People who do so cannot hope to receive any reward from the Father (Matthew 6:1-4). There are people who are very active in church and donate heavily for every church-related activity; but they also make sure that the congregation knows about their good works. An offering that is made to encourage others to notice us is not the kind of offering that is pleasing to God. In fact, it is not an offering to God if it is made with the purpose of developing a better reputation among a group of people.

We must remember that it is not that God, the creator, and owner of everything needs our offerings. He is just looking for individuals who are willing to share because they love Him and are aware that He has blessed them with everything they have. I love the fact that I do not have to bring a million dollars to gain my Master's recognition. When given with a gracious heart, the Omnipotent Lord of the Universe will stop to applaud the two copper coins presented by a widow (Luke 21:1-3). Abel offered to please God; he did not offer to look good in the sight of his family members. His thankfulness to God drove him to present an offering and that is why God appreciated his sacrifice. I wonder if God appreciates our offerings as He does that of Abel's.

God the Supplier

A man once came to me and said, "I planned to have a baby, but now I am having triplets. How am I going to feed all these kids?" I told him the Bible says to work and to be a father. If you are asked to fill up a truck, you fill it up faster than anybody else, and try not to move slowly to get through the eight hours. You don't spend time talking to your buddies and then take a lot of restroom breaks saying that you are praying to the Lord. Work is an active word; meaning to work until you hurt. Work is not working only to get a paycheck, but to have a testimony that you love God.

God says a man that doesn't work should not eat and when he does work he will eat (2 Thessalonians 3:10). Where in the Bible does it say that your job makes you eat? Rather, the Bible tells us to work and obey God so that God can be the supplier. His Word never says that by your work, He would feed you. Instead, it says that if you seek Him, He would feed you.

Maybe you are not able to see how your job is going to feed your family, but since He told us to work, just do it. Doesn't He take care of the sparrows and dress the lilies in the field better than Solomon? (Matthew 6:25-30)

Why do we worry about what we will eat, drink, and wear? I remember the time I was laid off for a year and I called my father and he told me to forget about the master's degree and go to work and live and be a man of God. I watched my family taken care of and I learned that it wasn't my work, but my faithfulness to God that fed me. Don't believe in the world system that says that if you do this, you will have that. If the

Lord does not bless you, you will work yourself to death and still will not be able to feed your family.

I was flying one day to Kansas City and I watched the airlines personnel trying to de-ice the plane by spraying it. They had two or three people working on the wings and the pilot was saying we have to get out of the airport fast. He told us to stay buckled, because if we stayed on the ground too long, the plane was going to ice again and the authorities would have to ground the plane. I was thinking "This is crazy! We are trying to take off with wings that are iced. Because the man told us to sit in the seat; we are sitting in the seat and securing ourselves with a little black seatbelt!"

How can people have this kind of faith to get into an iced plane, but cannot trust God to supply their needs? How can we say I don't believe I need to give to God, while all the time we are walking on His earth and use His atmosphere to even get up in the air? We find it easier to believe a man that is locked in the cockpit that we cannot even see; but claim that we have to actually see God before we believe Him. What if the pilot had some heart disease or had one too many before the flight? I was getting ready to preach on that plane. We were willing to trust a man on the radio, but God comes to us through His Word and we have the audacity to ignore Him.

When I went to Freeport, Texas, I really wanted to go deep sea diving, but my wife said that she was not ready to be a widow yet, so I decided to be still. I watched people come with tanks and masks, go under the water and breathe out of a tank, which they simply picked up, put on their backs, and jumped in the water--but they can't trust in God! I think about the many people who have direct deposit, call the automated system, and write their checks—but they don't trust in God to provide for their needs.

We have people on the Internet paying off bills with their account and credit card numbers into cyberspace, talking about firewalls and stuff—but they don't trust God as their supplier! We read all those labels on food items and act like we have taken each product to the lab to test if what the labels are claiming is actually true—but don't trust God! I am not asking you not to do any of the above. I just find it hard to accept that we can trust everyone and everything, but we just do not want to trust God enough to express our gratitude by laying our offerings at his feet.

We must realize that God is the same yesterday, today, and tomorrow. He is the King of kings and the Lord of lords. He is who created everything that your eyes can behold and even what is beyond your comprehension and understanding. So don't hold back when it comes to presenting your offerings to Him. There is no gift that can be too great—and there is no gift that He will consider too small if given with a pure heart. Get up from your comfort and lethargy and offer yourself to Him and your life will never be the same. A better sacrifice—aim for it and you will have the privilege of experiencing God's pleasure in your life!

CHAPTER 7

Don't Give Up

> *And a woman who had had a hemorrhage for twelve years, and had endured much at the hands of many physicians, and had spent all that she had and was not helped at all, but rather had grown worse, after hearing about Jesus, came up in the crowd behind Him and touched His cloak. (Mark 5:25-27)*

There was a man who sold everything that he had and decided to join the gold rush. He bought a little plot and he worked on that plot day in and day out, month after month in search of gold. He was able to feed his family as he worked on the plot—but he was never able to find gold. As months passed, his frustration grew. Every single day he would go home disappointed and angry, until finally one day he picked up a gun, shot his wife, his daughter, and himself.

The community was saddened by what had happened. Some folks decided to dig for one more day. During that same day, they found gold in large quantities. If that man had drilled for just one more day; all that he had desired, wished for, sacrificed for, and all that he had spent his life savings to accomplish would have come true.

Faith That Does Not Quit

Faith that produces reward is a faith that is persistent. Faith that produces reward is a faith that does not give up. It does not allow us to quit applying God's Word, when difficulties, obstacles, and issues come in our lives. It is a faith that presses, that makes us work hard. It is that faith, without which, it is impossible to please Him. (Hebrews 11: 6)

The Gospel according to Mark introduces us to a woman who had the kind of faith that refused to give up. We are told that this woman had been suffering from hemorrhage for several years and had been to every doctor in her day. She had spent all her money in her quest for healing. Yet nothing and no one had been able to help her. Moreover, she had such a problem that the community knew about her illness. In fact, we can safely assume that the crowd knew about her disease, because the Bible says the crowd was pressing in on Jesus. (Mark 5:31) The word "pressing" comes from winepress. In those days, when they wanted to make wine, people would go in bare feet and press on the grapes and squeeze the juice out. How did this woman make it to Jesus with all these people pressing against Him? They probably moved away from her as they did not want to touch her and become unclean, according to the Old Testament law, which stated: "When you touch a person that is unclean, you become unclean." (Leviticus 15:25-27)

Since she was considered unclean, this woman could never go to the temple. All her sins were piled up on her. She could not go to the priest because she never stopped hemorrhaging. She was unclean, unwell, tired, broke, in all likelihood--ostracized, surely--lonely, and considered sinful until she touched Jesus.

Think about it, she touched Jesus! And you can too; when you are willing to have the kind of faith that does not give up!

She heard and examined. Mark tells us that the woman, "after hearing about Jesus, came up in the crowd behind Him, and touched His cloak." (Leviticus 15:27) This woman's faith was awesomely productive, because she "heard." It is very likely that this woman could not go with the crowd to listen to Jesus, because nobody wanted to be around her. She could not go to the temple when Jesus taught there because she was unclean, but she could hear all the things that the people were saying.

In other words, she heard about Jesus, she heard about His miracles, and she looked back on Genesis to Deuteronomy. (She did not have Genesis to Malachi.) When she heard about Jesus, when she looked at the works He was doing, and she examined God's Word to understand what she heard. The word "hearing" means that when she examined Him against the standard, she had the conviction that Jesus is from God. That conviction drove her to Jesus Christ. She did not care what anyone said; she was going to press forward.

She tested what she heard. The Bible says, "Test the spirits." (1 John 4:1) When you hear a person speak, be like the Berean Christians (Acts 17: 11) and test what you hear, because you are responsible for what you hear. You are responsible for believing what you believe. If you believe the wrong thing, and if you do not have a deep conviction about the right thing, your faith will not produce awesome results.

Many of us like to listen to anybody and everybody and then we get frustrated and stressed out. You say, "Well, that preacher is a conservative and that one is a moderate and the other one is liberal." That is a worldly way of looking at God's Word. In the Bible, it is either the truth or it is a lie. There's no moderate, conservative or liberal in the Bible. They are either preaching the Word or they are not preaching the Word.

The Bible says, "Jesus is the way, the truth, and the life" (John 14:6). He is the truth. If you don't hold on to the truth, you will miss Jesus Christ. Since you can only do all things through Christ (Philippians 4:13), if you have missed the truth and you have missed Christ, you cannot do all things. Therefore, you cannot be productive and your faith is null and void. It is either a lie or it is truth. Some of you say, "Most of what he said is the truth." No single prophet from God speaks most of the truth. The prophet speaks the truth or is not a prophet. If you are mostly right and somewhat wrong, it is not the truth, because truth is completely and absolutely true.

In the first three verses of Deuteronomy 13, you learn some important lessons: "If a prophet or a dreamer." You know folks like to say, "I heard from God last night. While I was sleeping, God told me in a dream." Well, see if what they are saying matches with His Word. If it does not match with the Word, it was a good dream. I am glad it helped you to sleep well.

"If a prophet or a dreamer of dreams arises among you and gives you a sign or a wonder and the sign or the wonder comes true." They actually give you a sign that works--the person looks healed, the situation looks great--it works, it looks real. The Bible never said that

Satan does not perform signs and wonders. The Bible says that Satan is like the shining star. He imitates Christ. If Christ can heal somebody; Satan is going to try to heal too. If Christ can get somebody up, Satan is going to do the same thing, because he wants you to turn away from Jesus.

"Concerning which he spoke to you, saying, 'Let us go after other gods (whom you have not known) and let us serve them.'" This is a test. The test is not in the sign and wonder, because a sign and wonder is too subjective. You cannot test it. However, you can test his words, because you have from Genesis to Revelation. You see the signs. You see the wonders. It looks real, but you have to test what the dreamer is saying.

Some individuals like to tell you, "If you want money, you throw the money at me and God will throw it back at you." While God says in His word, "You want to be blessed, work hard, and serve me by giving me a tenth of that as thanksgiving and I will bless you in return." (Malachi 3:10-12) Others want you to worship other gods. God has said, "You shall have no other gods before me." (Exodus 20:3) Some folks are going to tell you to name it and claim it. When you name it and claim your blessings and you end up with a whole bunch of credit cards that keep claiming you, you know that that was not from God. Not everything that you hear comes from the Lord.

"You shall not listen to the words of that prophet or that dreamer of dreams." The verse is not asking us to be patient with them; rather it is saying, "You are responsible for what you listen." When they start teaching a lie on the television, you change the channel. It is your responsibility to do it, because the conviction you develop from a false word will give you false results. You shut it off. It's your responsibility. Don't hope the television will go off!

He says, "For the Lord your God is testing you to find out if you love the Lord your God with all your heart and with all your soul." He is going to have it on all the channels, all the radios, churches galore, people saying this, people saying that. He's testing you to find out if you are going to sit back like the Berean Christians and examine the Word. Get a Bible dictionary. Check it out and search for the truth. He has anointed you to know the truth (1 John 2:27). He has anointed you so that you, His sheep, will hear His voice and respond to His voice.

You may know that sheep are very particular. Goats eat anything. You put a banana skin in front of a goat and a goat will eat it. I am from South America, so I can tell you about a goat. Goats will eat anything. Sheep are very particular and have to be in green pastures. If they go through a valley that has a shadow cast on it, they think it is the valley of death and they have no means of protection or defense. Sheep cannot fight for themselves. A goat may hit you, knock you, or ram you, but a sheep is not able to defend itself.

When the sheep are going through a valley, the shepherd walks in front of them and makes sure that they don't run off. The shepherd knows that it is day, but because of the shadow on the valley, the sheep think that it is night and imagine that wolves are waiting to attack them. Sheep do not go where they think it is dangerous. That's why, sometimes if you don't have a nice air-conditioned church with soft pews--sheep don't come! God says, "You are my sheep. You should know my voice. Veer from Satan."

In fact, shepherds have a particular call for their sheep. They stand up and yodel and the sheep come running to them. As His sheep, do you go running to Him?

When I was working with the Urban Alternative ministry in Dallas, Texas, I used to travel a lot. Every now and then, my wife would tease me and say, "What makes you think I am going be here when you get back?" I would reply, "Baby, I treat you too good. I am the love of your life. I know you are going to be here when I get back. No matter where I go, how far I go, you are so in love with me that you will be waiting for me." Christ is saying, "When I am the love of your life, you will know my voice and come running to me."

There was a prophet during the time of Jeroboam. God told him, "Go to Jeroboam, and I want you to do this, but don't eat bread or drink water there, nor return by the way which you came." Prophet goes to Jeroboam, does all the great things and awesome things happen. An old prophet is told by his sons, "This prophet did great things from God." The old man said, "I got to go talk to that prophet." He goes and talks to the prophet. He says, "An angel spoke to me by the word of God saying that you must come to eat with me." That was a lie, but the prophet listens to him and goes and he eats with him. Then God really touches the old man and he tells the prophet, "Because you chose to do what God told you not to do, you, prophet, will die." That prophet died on his way back home. (1 Kings 13:1-25)

Many of us don't get the blessings of God, because somebody shows up and says, "God says." We don't go in the Bible to check it out, some of us respond: "Ooh, he sounds right," or "Ooh, that sounds good." We chase an idea, get committed to it, and we have deep convictions about it, but it doesn't produce results blessed by God and we get mad at God. God says, "If you believe a lie, you are responsible for it, and you bear the consequences of it. I just tested my love for you and you chose to be idolatrous."

There was a man who saw someone hang gliding, and he thought, "Man, that's pretty. I would love to sail through the sky." He talked briefly with the man who had been hang gliding and decided to jump off the cliff. In his haste, he forgot to ask the guy questions like, "What are the rules regarding hang gliding? How should one land correctly?" That seemed irrelevant for him. He just wanted to hang glide.

While he had been watching the other man, everything looked easy. and he thought he was going to just glide down slowly and beautifully. When he actually started hang gliding, that thing went down so fast that he crashed into some trees. He came back and said, "Man, I came down so fast I crashed. Where did I go wrong?" The other man replied, "I am learning too. I keep crashing at the same spot, and I cannot figure how to miss the spot!"

Many of us believe that we are deeply convicted and we like to jump into things. We jump into jobs believing, "If I do this, God will do this." We jump into marriage thinking, "If I do this, God will do this." We always jump into things, never achieving anything, and we end up crashing.

I was at a conference and there was a preacher who stood up with tears in his eyes and explained to us how he had messed up his daughter's faith. His daughter loved her godmother who was suffering from cancer. However, in the midst of a great, spirit-filled service, this preacher had claimed, "God told me that you are going be healed and you will not die." Two weeks later, this woman died.

His daughter came to his room knocking, "Daddy, you said that God has said that my godmother will not die. But Daddy, how could it be that you heard from God, who doesn't lie and my godmother died? How could that be?" He said he tried to talk to her, but the girl kept crying. One night he had to walk in there and confess to her, "Daddy lied. Daddy was deceiving and being deceived. I was saying some things because people like to hear some things. I lied, and what I said was not from God." Despite his explanation, his daughter continues to be confused about all that has happened.

People will want to hear all kinds of things, but remember, "All Scripture is inspired by God and profitable for teaching, for reproof, for correction, for training in righteousness; that the man of God may be adequate, equipped for every good work" (2 Timothy 3:16, 17). You don't need to run after somebody. You have the Word and it will equip you to do every good work. Follow the conviction of the Word of God, stick with that conviction, and you will be prepared for everything.

God's Word is not for games. That is why the Bible is called the cannon. Cannon is like a reed that grew in a swamp. The reed grew so straight that when a carpenter wanted to know if something was straight or bent, he used to take a reed and line it up against whatever he was doing. The Word of God is the cannon. It is straight, and when you measure your life against the Word of God, you will never go wrong.

What made this woman's faith productive? This woman listened and she tested what she heard. You have the Bible, test what you hear.

She sought Him. The woman did not hear about Him, examine and test what she heard and then walk away. She sought Him. "For she thought, 'If I just touch His garments, I shall get well' " (Mark 5:28). She had the kind of faith that produced action. True faith is an active faith, not a passive faith. That's why the Bible says, "If a man says he is just a hearer and he is not a doer, he miscalculates because he is not exercising faith" (James 1:22-24).

"And without faith it is impossible to please Him, for he who comes to God must believe that He is, and that He is a rewarder of those who seek Him" (Hebrews 11:6). As we have pointed out before, some people state, "Oh, I believe that Jesus walked in this earth and died on the cross." But then they don't seek Him during tough times. This woman sought Him. It did not matter what the people were saying. It did not matter how broke she was. It did not even matter that not a single physician was able to help her. Only Jesus mattered. All she wanted to do was touch His garment. She just knew that if she touched Jesus, she would be healed.

Think about this for a minute. All the people were pressing against Jesus. Why is it that their touch did not produce a positive response? The woman came with a level of faith that had heard, examined, tested and moved. You say, "But the disciples believed in Christ." It took Jesus 40 days to get them to really believe that He is Christ. Remember Thomas—he had to put his hand in Jesus' side, hand in Jesus' hand to believe that Jesus arose from the dead.

Many of us are like the crowd. We read the Bible. We go to church; we are willing to take notes. We hear the Word; we believe what it says. However, it does not produce any difference in our lives, because we don't seek Him with that level of faith and commitment that this woman had. If I were to tell you to grab a plug in this room, you will not be the same. Your life will be transformed.

When Christ comes into your life and you believe with a deep conviction, "God, this is the only way my marriage will work. I must do what you tell me. God, this is the only way my finances will get better. I will do what you tell me. God, this is the only way my job will be productive. I must do what you tell me." When you function with that deep commitment, it moves you to action. When you seek Him with that kind of faith, your life will never be the same.

The Result of Faith

This woman made her way to Jesus and when she touched Him, she was immediately healed (Mark 5:30). You don't see her shaking, falling over, frothing at the mouth. She touched Him and she was healed—immediately! Christ works like that. When your action causes you to seek Him, when your action causes you to move to Him, Christ responds. And when He responds, it's a done deal. Did the woman get the healing by herself? No. Did she do works to get it? No, but she made her way and she touched Him.

"And immediately, Jesus perceiving in Himself that the power proceeding from Him had gone forth, turned around in the crowd, 'Who touched my garments?' " (Mark 5:30). This is the verse that gets me excited. Her afflictions stopped, right then, and

Jesus perceived that the power--hold there. Does it say "a power"? No, no, no! At any point you see an article in front of a noun it is literally saying that that is special. Like He is "The Christ." There is no other Christ. When the Bible says "the power" there is no other power. It is not like He gave her a piece of His power or even some of the power. He gave her "the power." When Jesus fixes something, He gives you "the power." The Bible says that He has given us all a spiritual blessing. We don't lack anything.

When you get your home hooked up with the power-company, they give you some of their power. They don't give you all their power. If you go to the bank and borrow some money, they don't give you all their money. When you go to the doctor, the doctor gives you some medicine. However, when God starts to fix something because your deep conviction moves you to action, He says, "I am giving you all my power."

Notice it is not like He ran out of power. It is not like she took the power and He needed some more power. Jesus Christ perceived in Himself that the power had gone forth. He is still "the power" because He does not need electricity to keep His power; rather, He is the power plant!

This woman found a deep conviction, moved it to action, and she got "the power" as the result of her faith. When you come to Jesus Christ and you are broken and hurting and you need Jesus Christ to respond. When you need Him to come to you and answer the needs in your life. When you trust Him, wait on Him, obey His Word, despite your difficulty or hardship, and He responds, you don't get some power; you don't get a power; you need to know you get "the power." When you get touched with "the power" you don't only get things done, your life gets straightened and you become a new person!

Not only did the woman receive the power that healed her; she got a relationship that made her whole. The Bible says that He looked around to see the person who had done this. The disciples were saying, "Folks are pressing against you on all sides, and you are saying, 'Who touched me?'" (Mark 5:31) However, Jesus Christ was ignoring them. That verse in Greek means, "He was busy looking."

Why would Jesus look for somebody when He already knows where that person is? Jesus Christ could say, "Go to this village and get the donkey that I need to ride on" (Matthew 21:2). He already knew where the donkey was. Why does He want the woman to come forward? He wanted to initiate the process that would make her whole.

"But the woman fearing and trembling, aware of what had happened to her, came and fell before Him and told Him the whole truth" (Mark 5:33). Did she come fearing the doctors? I don't think so. Did she fear the crowd? That is irrelevant. She was aware of what had happened in her body and she fell before Him and told Him the whole truth. A deep conviction moves you to action. When that moves you to action, it should also move you to tell the whole truth.

Was the woman willing to trust Him and tell the whole truth? She didn't come to Jesus and told Him kind of what happened. She told Him everything. The Lord's Supper is also a time to tell the "whole truth." "God, I messed up this week. God, you know what I was doing. Lord, you know how I messed with those books. Lord, you know how I cheated; you know how I lied. God, I want to tell you the whole truth."

The woman fell to the feet of Jesus. He said to her, "Daughter," I love that; despite the crowd and the clamor, Jesus made this so personal. He called her, "Daughter!" "Daughter, your faith has made you well; go in peace, and be healed of your affliction" (Mark 5:34). "Your faith," not somebody else's faith in her, but her faith is what made her whole. "And now you don't have to live in shame; you can go to the temple. Daughter, you are well!"

Jesus lifted the woman, not just from her sickness, but from her shame and sorrow. The woman was no longer a woman with the flow; rather, she became the daughter of an ever-loving Father. Oh yes! This kind of faith results in a meaningful relationship with God and nothing can prevent you from having that relationship, because faith alone is needed to become a child of God. That's the kind of faith that makes a difference.

Daniel said, "I am convicted. I am convinced that the laws given by God are true. Everything spoken by Jeremiah is true. I don't care what they say. I don't care what they tell me to do. I am going to pray to my God." When Daniel was thrown in the lions' den, the king kept pacing through the night. Daniel did not pace; he just trusted God. The king came the next day, looked in the den, and said, "Daniel, get up out of there. We are going to worship your God." (Daniel 6) This is the kind of faith that brings awesome results.

There is no better example than Jesus. They tried to make Jesus Christ the king. "But Jesus Christ, you got the best welfare program in town. All you need is five loaves and two fish and you could feed us all. You have the best medical plans. All we need to do is come to you and you could heal us. Jesus Christ, you got the best deal. You can tell us how to find the money in the mouth of a fish. Let's make you a king." "You don't understand. I did not come to be a human king. I came to be the King of Kings." (1 Timothy 6:15)

"But Jesus Christ, you don't understand. We are going to spit on you and put a crown of thorns on your head." "I have come down from heaven, not to do my own will, but the will of Him who sent me." (John 6:38) "Jesus Christ, you don't understand. We are going to beat you with our fists. We are going to knock you down." "I am the Good Shepherd, and I lay down my life for the sheep so, therefore, beat me." (John 10:14-15) "But Jesus Christ, you don't understand. We are going to whip you so bad that you will see the pulp on your back." "You don't understand. I have already been to the Garden of Gethsemane and this is my Father's will for me." (Luke 22:42) "For God so loved the world that He gave His only begotten Son." (John 3:16)

Yes, they nailed Him to a cross, but early Sunday morning Jesus got up from the grave. Death had no power over Him; rather, all authority is given to Him in heaven and on earth." (Matthew 28:18) "Therefore also God highly exalted Him, and bestowed on Him the name which is above every name, that at the name of Jesus every knee should bow, of those who are in heaven, and on earth, and that every tongue should confess that Jesus Christ is Lord, to the glory of God the Father." (Philippians 2:9-11)

You want to see results--you need to have a true conviction that is based on the true Word. That's why Peter could say, "Oh yes, Christ, let them hang me upside down because my conviction is even deeper. I am willing to die for you." Paul could say, "It is not I who lives anymore. It is Christ that lives in me. The life that I now live, I live by faith in the Son of God." (Galatians 2:20)

I watched Michael Jordan play one time and he was having a bad game; missing one shot after another. You would think that after missing that many shots, he would quit, but not Michael Jordan. He kept shooting. The win came down to the last few seconds of the game and Michael Jordan took the ball. You would think that he would be scared to shoot the ball, because his team was losing by one point. You would think he would give it to somebody else, but not Michael Jordan. With a deep conviction believing he is one of the greatest basketball players, Michael Jordan took the last shot. Whoosh—his team won! Everybody at the end of the game talked about Michael Jordan; rather, than about the rest of the players that kept the team in the game.

Folks, Christ is saying: You may have missed your goal. You may have come to your marriage and made mistakes. You may have gone to your job and made mistakes. You may have gone through relationships and made mistakes. You may have managed your finances and made mistakes. However, when you hear about Christ, and you examine His Word, and you believe like this woman that He is from God and He is God, then He says you are ready to take that winning shot. And when you do that, you will experience "the power", which will bring forth awesome results."

Don't let anybody lie to you. You check it out, and when you are convinced that it is the truth, then you obey Him to the point of death, because He will never leave you.

Let your faith press on. Don't give up!

CHAPTER 8

Faith that Blesses

*And it came about while He was on the way to
Jerusalem, that He was passing between Samaria and
Galilee. And as He entered a certain village, ten leprous
men who stood at a distance met Him; and they raised their
voices, saying, 'Jesus, Master, have mercy on us!'*
(Luke 17:11-12)

A few weeks ago, as I was standing outside of a hotel in Atlanta, it dawned on me that I had no information about the person who was supposed to pick me up. I did not know the person's name, nor was I aware of the person's address or lifestyle. I did not know anything about the person, but I was going to let this person drive me to a church in order for me to speak that evening. I am not very familiar with Atlanta, so this person could have driven me to the backwoods of the city and I would have had no clue.

I continued to stand outside the hotel--not because I enjoy taking unnecessary risks in life--but because I had received a call during the week that said, "I am going to send somebody to pick you up. I will tell them to look for you, so you don't have to worry about looking for them." Now, that call was sufficient, because I trusted the caller. I know him as a man of integrity, a man who truly loves the Lord. Since I know the caller, and because of his word, what he said, and because of the fact that he had arranged for my ride, I got into that car and arrived at my destination and the evening was productive, because I trusted the word of somebody who is trustworthy. The evening proved to be a blessing to me, because I trusted the caller and accepted the ride.

Faith will Lead You to Jesus

We have repeated this time and again, and will continue to reiterate that faith blesses. Before you can enjoy that blessing, you have to find Christ and it takes energy to accomplish this step. I say that, we have to make an effort not because God is an elusive Father; but because we can only find Jesus when we are willing to off-load ourselves. The more you go after God; the more you have to deny yourself. That's when the work begins. We don't want to deny ourselves, so we push Him off. When we push Him off, we will not experience His presence.

A person came up to me and said, "You know, I really want to talk to you, but you are always too busy." I said to myself, "You are not looking for me hard enough, because I am in my office Monday through Wednesday. I answer calls, I return messages, and I meet people." Christ is saying when you are looking for Him, don't say, "Well, you know, God is busy." God is never too busy for you. "Well, I committed some sins this week." Confess it and keep searching. "Well, I am not a faithful church member." You know what to do, do it, and find Him.

Let's talk about the 10 leprous men. How do I know that the lepers were searching for Jesus? The

Faith that Blesses **117**

word "met" means that they were watching Him and were trying to catch up with Him. It does not say that they happened to bump into Jesus. You may know that these men could not come close to Jesus because they were lepers. They had to walk around saying "Lepers, lepers," so everybody could run away from them, because the disease was transferable and the lepers were considered unclean. Can you imagine how frustrating that must have been? That is why they stood at a distance from Jesus. The Bible says, "They met Him." They sought Him out and they knew exactly whom they were trying to meet, because they cried out, "Jesus, Master!"

We are so tired out by the world that we don't have time to find God. We have to watch our television shows. We have to work overtime. We have to go here and go there and by the time we come to the Bible study, we are snoring! On the other hand, these guys made an effort to find Jesus and their faith lead them to Christ.

Seek Him with passion and conviction and come to Him in unity. Look at the lepers; these men were a group of guys that had come together. These guys were friends in war. There were not only Jews in the group. There were Gentiles among them, because Jesus makes it a point to say, "this foreigner" (Luke 17:18), so this group included Gentiles and Jews and they came before Christ together.

God is saying that we must come in unity. If we don't come in unity, we don't get the kind of results we need. I don't care if you are Black, White, Asian or Hispanic, if you are a believer, that's enough. Until we work this out as a body, we will never have the kind of faith that pleases our Creator. You keep walking by each other, maybe not talking to each other, and that is not right. "A house divided against itself will not stand" (Mark 3:25).

"I do not ask on behalf of these alone, but for those also who believe in Me through their word; that they may all be one; even as You, Father, are in Me, and I in You, that they also may be in Us, so that the world may believe that You sent Me" (John 17:20-21). Jesus says that the world will not see God if they don't see us operating together. Where there is unity, there is strength. When we put aside our feelings and petty differences and focus on finding God together, then we experience the blessings of God.

Faith will Lead You to Obey

The Gospel according to Luke tells us that when the lepers cried to Jesus for mercy, He said to them, "Go and show yourselves to the priests" (Luke 5:14). There is an important fact about obedience. When you decide to obey God, it is not always going to make sense nor will it always fit logically. Understand what's going on here. They are being sent to the priests, because the priests were required to ascertain that a person was free from disease. Then the priests would allow them to go into the temple to sacrifice to God and have their sins forgiven.

Christ tells them, "Go to the priests." Nowhere in that passage does He say, "You are healed. Go to the priests." What did they ask for? Mercy! However, they have not experienced any healing yet. He did not say, "You are healed." So, why should they go to the priests? If they had not gone, they would not have experienced healing. We may come to church and hear the Word, but if we refuse to obey Him we will not experience His blessings.

God says, "Honor your husband." "God, have you ever lived with him? You want me to respect him. He doesn't even have a brain. I am only with him because of the kids." God says, "You don't understand. I want you to respect him." "Love your wife" "Love my wife? She cannot cook; she does not clean. She is never there for me. Thank God for television because that helps me to spend my time." "You don't understand. I want you to love her; I want you to cherish her. I want you to take care of her like you take care of your own flesh." God speaks to his children: "I want you to stay pure." "But that person is cute. Lord, you are in heaven you cannot see what I see on earth. I know you want me to be happy. You don't enjoy seeing your children suffer." And God says, "Don't disobey me."

Disobeying God is why families are falling apart. That is why there is just as much divorce in the church as there is in the world; because we are just as disobedient in the church as they are out there. A wife no longer respects her husband and a husband no longer loves his wife. Why are singles getting pregnant in the church? It is because we are not doing what we are supposed to do. We disobey God.

It made no sense for them to go to the priests, but they did so anyway. Because they were obedient, they received blessings. Don't rely on human logic. The Bible says, "Trust in the Lord with all your heart, and do not lean on your own understanding. In all your ways acknowledge Him, and He will make your paths straight." (Proverbs 3:5-6) What a wonderful assurance. Just acknowledge Him and He will make your paths straight.

Faith that Blesses **120**

I remember a tough time in our marriage--tough time. I said, "Lord, you know I have feelings too. I don't know what I have done wrong." You know how we get lamebrain at the right time, and we claim that we are not aware of anything. We were going through frustration and stress and we could not hold it together. I tried to spend time with my wife and talk through it, but nothing seemed to be working.

I was going on a trip and I was scared, "God, keep her here." I sat there worried and I realized that God did not want me to figure this out by myself. I believe that God wanted me to concentrate on loving and cherishing my wife. He wanted me to allow the Holy Spirit to solve our problem. During the next few months, I learned how obedience leads to blessings. By the way, I still don't know what the problem was even after all these years.

Faith will Lead You to Bless!

This next lesson is huge. Many of us are going to hear God's Word; we are going to be committed to it; we are even going to be obedient and follow His commands; and then we will walk away from Him. All 10 men listened to Jesus. They had to walk along the way in obedience to Him. It was only then that they started to heal. Only just one guy said, "Man, I used to have straps of cloth around my face, now my face feels so good, my hands are fine, and my feet feel great! I don't need to go to the priests. I need to go back and worship the One who healed me!" As we learned earlier with Abel, faith must always lead you to worship the Lord—your worship is an integral part of your relationship with God. Faith that moves you to bless the name of the Lord is the kind of faith that brings joy to the heart of the Lord.

Nowhere in this passage did it say that Christ told the men to come back to Him. Christ did not say anything. Yet this man decided to turn back. If you study this miracle in the Greek language, you realize that the author does not use the word "heal" for general healing. The author picks the word that means "God does the healing." This man is coming back to give thanks to Christ, the Lord.

He came back praising God with a loud voice. You think this man cared that he was being too loud? I don't think so! "Now, one of them when he saw that he had been healed turned back glorifying God with a loud voice, and he fell on his face at His feet, giving thanks to Him. And he was a Samaritan" (Luke 17:15-16).

He came praising and worshipping the Lord: "God, you are great. God, you are awesome. God, you are holy." To glorify God is to talk about His nature, His being, His power, and His omnipresence. It is to talk about who He is. This man is not a Jew. He is a Samaritan. "You are a God that loves everybody. God, I don't have to be rich, I don't have to be Black; I don't have to be White; I don't have to be a Jew. I can be a Samaritan and you still love me. God, I am a sinner; but you still love me. You are God. You are gracious; you are faithful." He is not embarrassed about his worship—he is sincere and loud!

However, God did not fix all his problems on that very day. Did God fix his home situation? No. The man did not have a job. He had been going through trash and garbage to get stuff to eat. He has been a total beggar and lived in abject poverty. Did Christ fix his finances? No. Did Christ fix his family relations? No. However, Christ did do one thing—He heals him, and that was enough for the man to turn back and worship Him.

Are you willing to say: "God, you know what, my marriage is not fixed all the way, but I have a deeper strength to deal with it. God, you know, I am still single; but I can handle myself better now. In some ways--even though I feel the pressure--I can better handle my kids. I know all my problems are not over, but I see you helping me to move on in life. God, though my finances are tight, I am giving to you, and somehow all my bills are paid. Dear Lord, when I truly consider my blessings they are countless. So God, I can't wait until they say, "Come to the house of the Lord and worship" (Psalm 122:1-4).

I wish God could see all of us walk like that. I wish all of us would have the kind of faith that blesses His name. People ask, "Why are the worldly people so blessed?" I am going to tell you why. Some of them don't come to church; but if somebody is hurting, they will write a check to help that person. Many non-saved people offer help when a tornado causes destruction in an area. A non-Christian man says, "Man, I am supposed to love my wife." He does it and his marriage becomes blessed. We then ask, "God, why are you are blessing him?" It is because he took a biblical principle, he applied it to his house, and it worked. God says, "My Word shall not return to me empty." (Isaiah 55:11) Did God say His Word should not return void for Christians? No. God's Word will not return void. Whoever picks it up and obeys, it will not return void. That is why many of them are blessed, and we are not. The Jews are heading to the priests; but the Samaritan, he is heading back to the Priest, Jesus Christ.

We forget to appreciate the things we have. "I had a bad week." But you forget you had a week. "I am having a bad day." But at least you are going through the day. "This car is barely working." At least you are not walking. "Look at this apartment. I wish I had a house." Thank God, you have an apartment. "God, look at my tiny house. I wish I had a bigger house like everybody else." Thank God, you have a house. "My money is not right." "I have to go home with this man and he is not right." "My wife is not right." God must fix everything, but God is saying, "Isn't caring for you, and loving you every single day enough?" What more must He do before we worship Him? This man ran back to Him--how about you?

Jesus answered, "Were there not ten cleansed? But the nine--where are they?" (Luke17:17) "Was no one found who turned back to give glory to God, except this foreigner?" (Luke 17:18) Jesus Christ was really trying to make a point here. He was around a bunch of Jews, traveling to Jerusalem. He said, "This foreigner has come back, but where are the other Jews. I know they have been healed. I know I healed them from their leprosy."

There are days when Christ asks the same questions about us. "I know I helped them miss an accident this week. I know I made them go back and check the door so they would not get in that wreck. I know I fed them this week. I know that they were broke, but when they went to that pantry, I made them see some stuff, brought some stuff to their mind that they did not think about before. I know I did that.

When their boss was thinking of firing them, I took them off the list. They were without a job and yet they had food to eat. I know that disease had entered their body and I plucked it out this week. Is no one willing to say thank you?"

Many of us are not blessed because we are very apathetic about worship. We have to have a perfect week before we come to church, or we have to have a devastating accident in our lives before we say, "God, help me." Usually we mumble, "Lord, I lay me down to sleep. Help my soul to go to sleep and to get up. Amen." Christ will not come on a Sunday morning and go, "Pow! Get up, time to go to church."

Every Sunday is not going to be a perfect weather day. He wants to know why is it that you claim to love Him, yet refuse to worship Him with thanksgiving. Why is it that you have food in your stomach and yet you have trouble praising Him? The Samaritan decided to bless the Lord. The decision to give praise is your decision. Jesus will not force you to worship Him. When you have a faith that blesses and lifts the name of the Almighty Lord, then not only do you receive blessings from God, but your life itself becomes a blessing.

Faith will Lead You to Wait to be Blessed

This man stayed at the feet of Jesus until Jesus told him to go his way. Jesus looked at him and said, "Rise and go your way, your faith has made you well" (Luke 17:19). Though Christ was yet to die on the cross and shed his blood for the sins of the world, Jesus knew that his kind of faith would lead this man to believe in Him at the cross. Once a leper, this man was now healed, restored, made whole, and blessed.

A person who doesn't come wholeheartedly to worship God will miss the blessing. Many of us hit the door before the benediction. Do you know that if you miss the benediction, you miss the final blessing? "Then Aaron lifted up his hands toward the people and blessed them, and he stepped down after making the sin offering and the burnt offering and the peace offerings. And Moses and Aaron went into the tent of meeting. When they came out and blessed the people, the glory of the LORD appeared to all the people" (Leviticus 9:22-23).

The same blessing that Aaron and Moses had, they shared that blessing with the people. When the people received the blessing; the glory of God was dispensed to the people.

Benediction is a time to be blessed. Benediction is also a time when God responds to our prayers after we worship Him. This is what they would say at the benediction during the Old Testament times: "The LORD bless you and keep you. The LORD make His face shine on you and be gracious to you. The LORD lift up His countenance on you and give you peace" (Numbers 6:24-26). When your faith keeps you at the feet of Jesus, it moves God to bless you abundantly.

Our family came to this country with nothing. All of us lived in a tiny apartment on Ferguson Road in Dallas, Texas. In our home, we had devotions. Going to church was never an option; we automatically got dressed to go. Our mother always told us, "May your faith in God guide your steps."

I remember going to an optometrist and telling her, "I don't have any money, but I need my glasses fixed. I cannot see things clearly without them. I am going to pay you, but I can't pay you now." The woman said, "If you are crazy enough to come in here and think I am going to give you glasses, you got them." I said, "Thank you, Jesus." I talked to the college authorities, "Listen, I don't have the money right now, but I am not leaving. I have been here three years. I paid you for three years. You are going to help me stay, because I am going to graduate." They said, "Paul, sit down. You are a good kid. We will take care of you. Let us work some things out; and we will set you up where you can take care of your tuition." I just blessed the name of the Lord.

I remember calling home and saying, "Mom, I think I am going to make it with God's help." She said, "I know you are going to make it because you don't need to have everything to experience the grace of God. All you need is God, and He's good enough for anybody. Take just one step of faith today and God will give you the strength for the next step. But never ever forget to bless the name of the Lord."

Indeed, "Bless the Lord, O my soul and all that is within me, bless His holy name" (Psalm 103:1).

May we have the faith that blesses!

CHAPTER 9

Faith that Rocks

"By faith Moses when he had grown up, refused to be called the son of Pharaoh's daughter; choosing rather to endure ill-treatment with the people of God, than to enjoy the passing pleasures of sin; considering the reproach of Christ greater riches than the treasures of Egypt; for he was looking to the reward." (Hebrews 11:24-26)

Suppose God decides to redirect your life. Will you follow Him even if you do not like the direction He is asking you to go? I have had the honor of meeting a gentleman in Nairobi, Kenya, who used to serve as a Baptist preacher over a considerable congregation of people. While he was pasturing, a war broke out and hundreds of thousands of people were killed and this pastor had to run to a refugee camp. While at the camp some individuals offered to host him with other pastors so he would not have to deal with tents, sleeping on hard ground, and outdoor restrooms. This great pastor responded, "No, wherever my people go I will go, wherever they suffer I will suffer; my ministry is no longer in the church house, but in this refugee camp."

In fact, he decided to hold church in the refugee camp and love and serve the people as he lived in their midst. He understood that God had redirected his life by allowing situations in his life where he could no longer do the things he was accustomed to doing. He decided to remain faithful to God by helping people from tent to tent. He made the decision that since God had allowed trials to take place in his life, he would go through difficulties, pastor in the environment that God had placed him in, and be blessed by God. To this day, this man serves not only as a pastor to his people, but also ministers to pastors, leaders and churches to ensure that what happened in his native land does not happen in any other country in Africa.

Augustine once said that if you believe what you like in the gospel and reject what you don't like, it is not the gospel you believe in, but yourself. If we believe in the Word when it is convenient and then drop it when it is not, we believe in ourselves and not in God, and we surely cannot claim to have a faith that rocks.

Life's Comfort or God's Direction

The Bible tells us that God placed Moses in a situation where he was able to have a taste of wealth, education, and an extravagant lifestyle. However, at the age of 40, he had to decide if he wanted to continue being an Egyptian or set aside everything and claim his Jewish heritage. It is crucial that we understand that Moses was about to become a Pharaoh. Do you know that several thousand pounds of pure gold were found in one Pharaoh's tomb? Moses would have had all the riches available to him, since he was poised to become the master of the mightiest nation of the world at that time.

In fact, the Egyptians wielded the same influence that the Americans hold over the world today. To be a Pharaoh of Egypt meant that Moses would not only be wealthy, but also extremely powerful. In fact, Moses would have been viewed as a god. People would have come to him and bowed to him and all his whims and fancies would have been fulfilled. Not only would Moses have money and power, but as Pharaoh he could also have any woman that he wanted.

I guess it would be safe to conclude that Moses had everything a person would want, but I love the fact that Moses found it impossible to ignore God's redirection for his life. We have to understand that faith will affect our purpose in life. Faith does not allow us to be the same old Americans. Moses learned that if he was going to lean on God, his purpose would change. His purpose to be Pharaoh disappeared; his purpose to be a Jew was now in place.

Interestingly, we actually follow a system just like Moses would have followed that has a whole educational section to it that violates God's Word. A key word to know is *cosmos*, which means an organized force that is directed against God. It means the world teaches contrary to the teachings of God. The world tells us that we don't need anyone and that we ought to build ourselves up by our own bootstraps. If we cannot even breathe without the grace of God, how can we claim to build our lives without the help of our Creator? People will come to church and say they don't need anyone; they come to listen and then do exactly what they want to do. Moreover, they don't want to be bothered with anyone and they don't realize that this is an Egyptian mentality.

God tells us to love our neighbor as ourselves and when He talks about neighbor, He does not just mean the people that live next to you. The word *neighbor* means anyone in your vicinity. For example, when you stop at a traffic light; the person in the car next to you is considered your neighbor. The person in the cubicle next to you at work is considered your neighbor. The Bible says anyone that comes in close proximity with you is your neighbor and challenges us to love the Lord our God with all our heart, soul, and mind, and to love our neighbor as ourselves. The world teaches us to ignore the hurting souls and unlike the Good Samaritan think only about ourselves.

It is very important that we know that everything the world teaches without the Bible is a lie. A lie is about nonexistence. If I was to go outside this building and say the reason why these cars are here is because people have stopped here to catch the bus to go downtown for a Rockets game. When you go downtown to investigate, you will see that the buses are lined up, but not the people, because there is no game today. Looks like I told a lie! A lie is a circumstance that does not exist and this is why people have to tell lies to cover earlier lies.

People who lie are actually trying to make something be something that does not exist. Anytime you have to create something, you have to build it yourself. We are not beings that can create anything. The more we try to create something, the more we have to lie, because we don't have any truth to back it up. This is why; to believe anything the world says that has no biblical truth is to believe a lie. As a result, we believe in nothing. It should not surprise us that faith is substance. because faith is about truth and truth is based on evidence. Truth is not something you have to create, it has already been created and because of that, it is something you can trust.

If we choose to demonstrate traits of faith this world will change. The world tells us that two consenting adults can stay together without getting married. The Bible says that our body is God's temple and no one can touch our body unless they follow God's rules. (I Corinthians 6: 12-20) He made our bodies out of the dust of the earth; He breathes into them, feeds them, raise the sun; and provides oxygen for our lungs; therefore, this body belongs to God. As our Creator, He wants us to take care of our body, although the world tells us that we have a right to submit to our desires. Sadly, since we prefer to remain adamant, many diseases are taking over and eventually our body is destroyed. Satan knows that all he has to do is get us into his world system and we will face destruction in our lives.

Dear friend, before you were born, God decided whether you are going to be male or female. He knows everything about your life—and the length of your days on this earth. He wants to use you as a testimony. God put you on your job so that others who are not coming to church will get to see how Christians look, act, and behave. People who don't even believe in the Bible or even hear about the Bible can see how people act when pink slips are being distributed. They would see how loving we are to our spouses and children. They would see what it is like to respect an unjust boss or how Christians respond when someone maligns them. They would see the biblical handling of money and possessions.

God used Moses as powerful testimony in the midst of an unbelieving nation. Please note two very important words that defined Moses' decisions. Hebrews 11:24 says that Moses "refused" to be called Pharaoh's son and verse 25 tells us that Moses "chose" to endure ill treatment with the people of God?

When Hebrews talks about refusing and then choosing, we have to understand that one is a mental choice and the other one is a functional decision. If we refuse something, we have just distanced our self from someone or something. When we choose something, we have meticulously evaluated everything and decided to go a different way. Moses had to make a choice and he decided to take the path to eternal life. Today, if you have the choice to follow the world's system or God's system, what path are you going to take? Are you ready to accept His redirection for your life?

Choosing to Endure

Moses chose to endure ill treatment with the people of God; rather than enjoy passing pleasures of sin. It is quite possible that Moses looked at his life in Pharaoh's palace and said, "What is the point. They say if I become a Pharaoh, I'll have the good life. I'm watching Pharaoh and he actually doesn't have a good life. He is going from woman to woman and he is still not content. He has all the money and he is still lonely." Moses must have realized that Pharaoh does not have a good life. On the other hand, Moses may have thought, "My mama had to give me up, but she faithfully taught me. She is excited about the same husband that she has had for years. I watched my mother take care of my brothers and sisters and they

Faith that Rocks **133**

love me more than Pharaoh's family ever could. The Pharaoh family is too busy fighting to see who is going to be in power."

We all understand that change is not always easy or comfortable. When Moses walked away from Egypt, it meant walking away from wealth, women, and comfort to a life of bare necessities. In fact, in the book of Hebrews, the author talks to a group of people that were tempted to go back to Judaism and forsake Christianity. Since Christians were losing their properties, being mocked, and put in prison; it seemed alright to go back to the easy way of living. It is during these times that we must remember patriarchs like Moses, who refused to give up.

Many people say that they need to follow God, but they never choose to walk in His ways. They claim that what God is teaching is right, but don't want to actually do what He says. "I am single and lonely and there are no guys talking to me right now that are saved and I would really like to be with somebody." Every time we decide to turn away, we go back to being an Egyptian. That is why it is important to remember that Moses chose to endure; which means to bear under whatever comes and to do what God commands.

God told Paul to preach the good news to the Gentiles. Paul experienced beatings, endured shipwrecks, was thrown in jail, and beaten and stoned. With the help of God, he chose to endure and all generations will remember how God used him in the days to come. Mary Magdalene, an ordinary woman from whom Jesus had taken out seven demons, chose to stay around the tomb and was the first to meet the risen Jesus. (Mark 16:9)

Joshua was asked to do one of the strangest things that I have heard. He was asked to walk around Jericho with his men seven times. (Joshua 6) In the situation that Joshua was facing, you would imagine he'd need a tank or a bulldozer—it definitely did not make sense to walk around a wall and blow a trumpet. They chose to endure according to the will of God and when they blew the trumpet the wall tumbled down and they witnessed a miracle. Surely, we have to be willing to endure if we are going to be effective in our lives. Our unwillingness to endure, once we make the decision drives us back to being the way we were.

There was a football player who was picked by a team, got cut, picked by another team, and then cut again; but he kept going. One day he finally got picked for a team. He was very excited, until one year later he was cut from that team, too. He was able to play with yet another team for three years and then he was cut again. Someone asked him why he was putting himself through such uncertainties, trying to make a life in different cities with new teams, especially knowing that he may be removed at any point. The guy responded, "I know I am a good player and some team will continue to pick me up because they have been picking me for nine years. So, therefore, even if I am removed from a team I am willing to endure knowing that my phone will ring and I will again be able to play the game I love."

When we walk with God, there are times when we may feel like He is not listening, and we feel like we have been cut. The Bible challenges us to endure and trust the evidence that is there. This guy had nine years of evidence and this helped him to remember that he will get picked again. You may feel discouraged and beaten down, but God is going to send somebody at the right time, to say hey how are you doing. Sometimes you feel like the world is coming to an end, but you come through the front doors of the church and God places a sermon on the pastor's heart that gives you direction for the particular situation that you are going through. Sometimes you feel you do not have the strength to do anything and God gives you the strength to stand up.

God is saying when you have that kind of evidence every single day of your life; you should endure knowing that God has always been there to pick you up. (Hebrews 12:1-2) And so, since I have been picked up over and over again and I stand convicted by the evidence that God is able to do exceedingly and abundantly above all that I could ask or think. Therefore, I can exercise faith, because it is the substance of what I have hoped for. I can endure on the basis of my past relationship with God that assures me that He will do it again.

Understanding Reward from the Father

Moses chose to leave behind Pharaoh's system that was hollow and decided to go after a godly-system based on truth. Moses evaluated the facts that were in front of him and decided to do something about it. Hebrews says, "Considering the reproach of Christ, greater riches than the treasures of Egypt; for he was looking for a reward." (Hebrews 11:26) You know it is hard to endure something when there is no reward.

We live the way we live, because we believe that God is going to bless us. The Bible says that our hope for reward gives us the ability to endure our hardship. Runners run the race knowing that there will be an end.

We go to work knowing that we will get off and are then able to relax; otherwise we will get depressed from doing the same thing every day. No one drives a car without knowing his or her destination. A lot of young people get in the car and say they are just riding, but they are still looking for something. The Bible says that when we walk by faith and stay focused on the reward it gives us the strength to endure.

If I share the gospel, the Bible tells me that when I arrive in heaven I will wear white garments and a crown. The Bible tells us that if we suffer for righteousness, He will bless us. God says He will guarantee the blessing, but we must do what God wants us to do. Peter exhorts us to gird our minds to action (1 Peter 1) and Paul testifies that if God is for us who can be against us (Romans 8:31).

Trials may come in the ring of life and knock us around a couple of times, but they can't knock us out. As I have said before, when God blesses us through His sovereign will and grace, no one can take away the blessing. It is exciting to know that God doesn't have to have what He is going to give us, before He gives. He can create it out of nothing. While you are sleeping, God can create a job or a promotion for you. He has the power to keep that raggedy car running. We may wonder how to pay the bills and God can choose to send money in some way. Sometimes, we are not expecting to be blessed and something comes in the mail saying that we overpaid something. We had no idea we overpaid, but God made sure the check came when we needed it the most. You may have gone to the tax office thinking you have to pay taxes and God allowed you to get money back. God knew we would need it and if He had given it to us earlier, we would have spent it. He saved it for when we needed it the most.

We have to understand that when we talk about rewards, it does not mean that things will work out just the way we want. God has a choice as to how He blesses us. Some people give up on God when He does not deliver the blessings their way. Instead of holding on to Him, we tend to pout and frown and complain that we had faith for nothing. Some turn away to experience joy through other means and have moments of happiness. However, those moments of happiness, may turn to trouble, because passing pleasures pass away quickly.

There are a lot of people who tell others to touch this, smell this, or grab this and everything will work out. Many do as they are told. If you are hoping for something that is not based on Scriptures, you do not have faith. What you have is false hope. Faith means having confident expectation based on His Word. Indeed, we should never expect something that is not based on His Word. When we expect something that has nothing to do with Him, He will not work on our behalf.

For instance, nowhere in the Bible does it say that: if I do everything right, my children will be perfect, or if I have faith, I will win a lottery; or He will make me a millionaire; and if you are single, He will get you a husband. Nor does He tell us that when we get married, we will be happy. We go into marriage expecting that response, because we are actually living on faith that is world-based. We feel it is all right to let our eyes wander and have a little fun in the night club and then expect God to deliver. That is not faith; that is convenience.

I am not saying that God will not bless you with a great marriage or financial security. He may choose to do so in His sovereign will. Most importantly, you must understand that though He may choose to reward us with different gifts and blessings, He has promised that He will never forsake us and His grace will be sufficient for our trials. We should aim to grow and equip ourselves to become people of God so that we can experience not only earthly blessings, but also the awesome power of God in our daily lives.

Fear and Punishment!

Moses in Exodus 2:14 saw two Hebrews fighting and asked them why they were fighting each other, since they had the same background and faced similar struggles as slaves. Surely, it does not seem right to fight a person that needs to be rescued and to hurt one's own brother. The men respond to Moses, "Who made you prince or judge over us?" In other words, they were telling Moses, "You are not one of us, you are a Pharaoh."

Well, Moses went out and killed the Egyptian who was abusing an Israelite. He wanted to prove his commitment to God and to His people by defending the Hebrew. Moses believed that his actions would draw his people to him and they would feel great knowing that they have someone of power and influence on their side. Unfortunately, the people turned against Moses and refused to acknowledge him as their leader. Since the king was also trying to kill him, Moses had to leave Egypt and take care of sheep in the wilderness for the next forty years.

Was God punishing Moses? No! Remember, God had told Abraham that for 400 years He was going to

Faith that Rocks **139**

let the children of Israel remain in Egypt. Moses was trying to get ahead of the schedule and God moved him out into the wilderness for 40 years, because it would not be until the 400th year that God would release them. God is saying to Moses that you can't rush me and make me do this on your time--it will be on my time.

It is imperative that we know that Moses did not leave Egypt because of fear; he left because he had made a decision for God. "By faith he left Egypt, not fearing the wrath of the king; for he endured, as seeing Him who is unseen." (Hebrews 11:27) If Moses had left Egypt because of fear, it would mean that he did not have faith. If your actions are controlled by fear, it means that you do not stand on firm ground. Until we allow the Spirit of God to take over and actually do what God says without waving fear in His face, we will not experience His power. If you think and say, "Man, if I go to work trying to be a Christian around all these unsaved people, they are going to try and take advantage of me," you are exercising fear and have run away from God. To look at something, evaluate it, and then walk away is fear. Fear is not always trembling; rather, it is to look at something, knowing it is the right thing to do, but choosing to go a different way.

God has a way of letting things come near us, because He wants to see if we are all about faith or fear. In fact, many times God will force us to demonstrate an act of faith, by letting us get backed up and not having a place to go. You have called everybody in the family and asked for money and they say," Make this the last time, because they are broke themselves." Now your back is against the wall, because you have no one to call and you are scared.

The Bible says that fear will kill a person's faith, because fear is to rely on our own ability to evaluate the circumstances based on our limited understanding. Each time this is done, fear controls our lives. When we act in fear, we miscalculate our actions and expect God to be and do certain things that He will not do. However, the Bible also says that when individuals act in faith and trust in the Lord with all their heart and choose to believe in God in spite of what they feel; they take the first step to productivity because fear is not dominating their decisions.

Of course, since we are imperfect beings, there are times when we all flounder. Acts tells us that "Moses was educated in all the learning of the Egyptians, and he was a man of power in words and deeds." (Acts 7:22) Moses knew politics, math, and science, and all there was to know about the Egyptians. He was trained to be a fluent speaker. Yet, when he met God in the wilderness and was asked to lead the Jews to freedom, he fumbled and looked for excuses and asked God to find someone else to do the speaking.

Not surprisingly, God got mad at him because Moses could speak. Moses had to be trained to be a powerful speaker, because he was expected to draw all the citizens and speak to them. God was giving him the same assignment, to draw all His people and speak to them. Moreover, God was sending Moses with His power. Moses allowed doubts to overtake his confidence. How awesome is God's love for us for when we remain in God, He is willing to take even our questions and imperfections and use them for His glory!

Growing Up

In Acts and Exodus that when Moses was 40, he grew up. In our culture, when individuals turn 18, they are considered grown. Technically and biblically the child is not grown at 18, age has nothing to do with it. In the Bible, when a child is grown, he is able to move out and take on whatever responsibilities an adult is supposed to have, with no dependence on the parents.

In fact, during biblical times, a son was considered grown only when he was able to move out and get a wife, because the husband was expected to build a house for his wife. Have you come across individuals that will tell you that you cannot correct them because they are twenty? Well, let me tell you, the child is acting like an American, but not as a Christian. A young man told me one day, "Man, I am grown. I'm twenty-two years old." I asked him where he lived and he said with his mama. He is not grown if he is still living with his mama.

Your child is grown when he or she has arrived at his or her best. The best does not mean what you want them to be, but what God wants them to be. We have too many people acting grown up and wanting the privileges of being grown up, but are either clueless or prefer to ignore the responsibilities that come with being an adult.

The Legacy

After 40 years, God took Moses back to Egypt and performed wonderful miracles by raising frogs and killing them, raising locusts and killing them, turning the Nile into blood and changing it back to water! Was God performing these miracles simply to impress everyone? No, it was because the Egyptians worshipped the frogs, cattle, and the Nile. God was trying to show the Israelites that He is the omnipotent God who has the power to destroy and give life.

It is interesting to note that Pharaoh went back and forth between yes and no and that it was not God who hardened Pharaoh's heart. Ephesians 4 says that when individuals say no to God over and over again, their hearts become hard and He cannot work in our lives, because He has given us the gift of free will. When people say yes to God they renew their minds and God transforms their lives. If our life remains fleshly, our hearts become hard towards God. You can preach to a carnal person till you are blue in the face, but they will not care about a word you are saying. Sadly, what happened to Pharaoh can happen to any of us, if we keep saying no to God. Beware of hardening your hearts and keep your ears tuned to His voice so you may not leave a legacy of hardened heart and wrong choices for those you love.

God told Moses to go and kill a lamb and to eat unleavened bread, which is bread without yeast, for seven days. God was telling the Israelites that it is God who made their release possible from Egypt and not something that the Israelites achieved on their own.

When you put yeast in the bread, it rises to make a nice loaf of bread and you can actually have more to eat. The Bible is saying you don't have plenty, because of anything you have done so take the yeast out because everything that has happened is the result of the power and grace of God!

Notice that God commanded the Israelites to celebrate the Passover meal. Moses, by faith, decided to do exactly what God said. Today, when we eat the Lord's Supper, we cannot ignore the Passover. The blood on the door-post represents the blood on the cross. The blood on the door-post protected the Jews from the angel of death and the blood that Jesus shed protects all believers from eternal hell. Moses was true to God's commandment during a time when Pharaoh, with his army, was mad at him. He was faithful he left the legacy of the Passover for generations to come.

Do you know that faith does not just bless us, but also those around us? This is the power of faith. We must understand that we may sit in church today, because our grandma or mother took us to church even when we didn't want to go. They may even have made us read our Bible and memorize verses, because they believed in passing their faith to their children. So many times, we are able to stand firm in our faith, because our ancestors trusted that God would bless them in His time. We know that they did not turn their backs on God in the midst of turmoil and sorrows.

We go through hectic times today and we often say that we don't have time for church. In the midst of our tiredness, what kind of legacy are we leaving for our children? What kind of heritage do we give our children when we are having a difficult time and want to get a divorce? We are telling our children that the way to solve problems is to split up, not because of adultery or abuse, but because it is the easy way out. Our kids are watching us, so when we walk, let us walk by faith. When we are at home or at work, act in a way that glorifies God. When God's timing is not the same as our timing, don't get tired and walk away. Hold on to His love and you will move from being an ordinary person to an extraordinary person of faith and you will be called blessed.

The role of Moses' mother always amazes me, because all throughout Exodus 2, we see how his mother found a way to take care of him and teach him. When Pharaoh's daughter wanted someone to come and care for the child, I believe that Moses' mother didn't just change his diaper, she taught him. She gave him the Word of God. She told him about Abraham, Isaac, and Jacob and why he was in Goshen. She taught him why the nation was there for over 300 years. In spite of the fact that Moses was getting an education from the Egyptians; he received life-changing education from his mother. Moses' mother taught him the Word of God.

Perhaps if Moses had not received an education from his mother, he would have remained an Egyptian. Perhaps because he heard the truth from his mother, he decided not to be an Egyptian. Acts 7:23 says, "When he was approaching the age of forty it entered his mind to visit his brethren, the sons of Israel." How did this enter his mind? It entered his mind because his mother had been teaching him, which helped Moses to run the race that God had set for Him.

I am able to serve the Lord today, because of the role my mother played in my life. She is not someone that you know or will read about in the papers or see on the television. She is not popular or someone great; but four of her eight children are in full-time ministry, because she chose to get up at 6:00 o'clock in the morning and teach her children the Word of God. She is an ordinary woman that chose to share God's love. She will be blessed in heaven because she took the time to walk by faith.

I have seen my mother go to the pantry and create food. I remember standing there with her asking where the food was and she would say that God would provide. I saw a woman that stood over the stove and prayed to God and we would never go hungry. Later when difficulties arose in my life, I trusted in the Lord and knew that He is my shield and my strength.

When I was in ministry and didn't getting paid for three months, I trusted God to do the same thing for me that He did for my mother and He has never failed me. Indeed, if we are going to be people with a legacy worth leaving behind, we have to make our lives all about faith. We must realize that our testimony will not only empower people around us, but also generations that follow in the coming years.

Faith that Rocks!

This is why the Bible tells us that we need a faith that rocks. We need a faith that makes a difference in the lives of other people. Are people growing closer to Christ by watching us? What exactly would people say if they were not lying about us at our funeral? Would they say that it was all about our money, the person we were dating, our car, and other material things that we had in our lives? If we didn't leave the mark of Jesus Christ in someone, the Bible says our lives were not all about faith. Rather, it was all about the stuff of America and these things don't go to heaven!

In Exodus, the people of Israel had been released from Egypt. God allowed them to wander in the wilderness and while they were wandering; the Egyptians came to Pharaoh and complained that Pharaoh had released their free labor. Pharaoh decided to go after the Israelites with a powerful army. God could have destroyed the army long before they reached the Israelites.

The Bible says that He allowed them to come near His people. In fact, God allowed Moses to take the children of Israel to the Red Sea and He made sure that they had no place to run. As soon as God put the Israelites against the wall, they decided that they did not want God; rather, they wanted Pharaoh. Frankly, many people go back to being Egyptians when their backs are up against the wall. It is because they would rather focus on Egypt instead of God!

Moses told the people not to fear and to stay quiet. Remember anytime we make a decision based on our own sense, the Bible calls it "fear." Moses did not make decisions based on his competence. He encouraged the people to stand by and see the salvation of the Lord that He had planned for them. (Exodus 14:21) Moses tried to get them to understand that the more they talked, the more frightened they would be.

Instead, when God is doing the working and the fighting, it is better to stand still and hear from Him. The minute we decide to take over, we get in the way of what God desires to do. God wants to speak to us, but we will not stop talking. It always amazes me that we even have something to say when God is speaking. When our boss speaks, we become quiet because we want to keep our jobs. Why is it when God speaks, we prefer to debate? We think that because we have been quiet and heeded God's instruction that He is going to operate tomorrow. God has His timings and His plans are perfect.

Going back to the Red Sea, God did not bring in boats or ships to provide an escape, neither did He bring armies and weapons to fight a battle; instead He told Moses to take a stick and hold it over the water. After being quiet, we must be still before God. Moses stretched out his hand over the sea and the Lord swept the sea back by a strong east wind all night (Exodus 14:21. Have you ever wondered why it took the omnipotent God all night to open up the Red Sea? God is saying be still even if your enemy is in your face because vengeance belongs to the Lord.

God tells us to keep doing what He has instructed us to do and He will deliver us in His time. He will change what needs to be changed if we choose to put our faith in Him and not in our own actions. I have often wondered why God opened up a path and not just dry the whole sea. I believe that He wanted the people to see that when they put their faith in Him, their enemy will not be able to come back up and breathe when He's done with them.

Indeed, Pharaoh's army died in the waters that came rushing back as soon as God's people had crossed safely to the other side. If the Israelites had fought the Egyptians, they might have won, but many would have lost their lives. With God's plan, the Jews didn't have to lift a finger and were able to head to the Promised Land.

I remember sitting in my office thinking how our expenses, because of a new building we had built, had gone from $5,200 to $16,000 in one year. I was questioning how we were going to resolve this problem when God told me to just shut up because He knew what He was doing. I started thinking in my heart that I wanted a Christian school and I began to thank Him for putting godly people in the school system. Four years later, the school opened and is doing better than our expectations.

There are times when you cannot see the evidence of faith and the things hoped for, but when we put our faith in what God says, we give Him room to be God. When we take over and try to fix everything, we are refusing to be still or quiet and we push God to the back seat. God is saying whenever we are ready, He will move into the front seat and drive. He has promised not to leave us or forsake us. He is in the car, but He is waiting for us to get out of the driver's seat.

A story is told about a man whose kids kept bugging him all day to take them ice skating, but he was nervous about them skating on a frozen lake. Since the kids kept pestering him, the dad finally gave in and told them to get dressed and get everything they would need to skate. When they reached their destination, the father told his children to sit on a bench near the lake and watch him as he skated. The excited kids couldn't believe that their daddy was skating without them. The dad started jumping and spinning around on the lake and in the process fell several times. The kids kept laughing at him, but he would get back up and skate again. The frustrated kids complained to their mother that their father was not letting them have any fun. Their mother looked at her kids and said, "Your father is ice skating and jumping, because he wants to make sure that there are no cracks and the ice is safe before he lets you all on it. Your daddy is going through the embarrassment and listening to you fuss while ensuring that you do not get hurt."

Truly our heavenly Father is the author and the finisher of our faith. Knowing that Satan creates havoc in our lives, He went ahead of us and started skating.

He jumped on the cross and took a beating and wore a crown of thorns on His head and a spear in His side; all because He wanted us to be safe. We keep saying God why are you taking so long? However, we must be still and let the Lord skate ahead of us to make sure that Satan does not have victory over our lives. Therefore, when we go out to skate we can laugh, talk, and perhaps even fall down, but not fall through the cracks. We can walk in the joy of the Lord because he has checked every part of the lake.

The father eventually allowed the kids to skate after sometime, but he kept watching them and he was never far from them. Jesus says though at times it may feel like He is not close by, if we sincerely look for God, we will find Him very near to us and we can grab hold of Him. God is saying He will never go far from us because He loves us. However, it is critical that we skate on the rink He has built for us and not develop our own rink. When we build our own rink, we are at our own mercy. When we skate on the rink that God has built, which is His Word from Genesis to Revelation, He has already run the course of the lake and it has passed His test.

Surely we can move mountains if we just rely on God when He speaks. People say to me, "Why doesn't God change things today like He did with Moses?" We have to realize that God doesn't have a Moses. People ask why doesn't God take care of their enemies like He did with Joshua? Quite simple, we have to be a Joshua. We have to stop asking God to be more when He is all that we need Him to be.

There is not a lack of God today. The truth is there is a lack of faith that rocks today. How could 12 people turn the world upside down and thousands of individuals are unable to impact a community at the level that would make it so powerful that people would have to recognize Christ in our lives. It is not because God needs to be more God; it is because we are refusing to become His children of faith. Instead, we are allowing Egypt to determine our worth.

Come let us pray that you and I will develop a faith that rocks. And as you pray, remember, we cannot stay stuck on the seat because it is more comfortable. Also remember that we must get up from the bench and skate on the ice only when God tells us to skate.

May our faith rock!

CHAPTER 10

Living Life with a Punch

But even if I am being poured out as a drink offering upon the sacrifice and service of your faith, I rejoice and share my joy with you all. And you too, I urge you, rejoice in the same way and share your joy with me.
Philippians 2:17-18

God wants you to live your life with a punch. He came to this earth that you might have life and might have it abundantly. (John 10:10) Yet our jobs, marriages, finances, daily problems, and our own disobedience wear us out. Don't let friends, family members, or even movies determine your life. Let God determine your life. "For I know the plans I have for you," declares the Lord, "plans for welfare and not for calamity to give you a future and a hope." (Jeremiah 29:11)

Paul went through some difficult times. He himself testifies that he was afflicted on every side. (2 Corinthians 7:5) "Five times I received from the Jews thirty-nine lashes. Three times I was beaten with rods, once I was stoned; three times I was shipwrecked, a night and a day I have spent in the deep. I have been on frequent journeys, in dangers from rivers, dangers from robbers, dangers from my countrymen, dangers from the Gentiles, dangers in the city, dangers in the wilderness, dangers on the sea, dangers among false brethren; I have been in labor and hardship, through many sleepless nights, in hunger and thirst, often without food, in cold and exposure." (2 Corinthians 11:25-27)

Paul who was once rich and well-respected, as to the Law a Pharisee, a Hebrew of Hebrews, of the tribe of Benjamin (Philippians 3:5-6) decided to walk with God and people stoned him, threw him outside the city, and wanted to kill him. Yet Paul could pray and sing hymns of praise to God after being beaten by rods and imprisoned in jail (Acts 16:22-25). Paul said, "I have learnt to be content in whatever circumstances I am" (Philippians 4:11). When you read about Paul, do you wonder--despite all his afflictions, how does Paul live his life with a punch? How does he enjoy abundant living in the midst of his sorrows? What keeps him going when the going gets tough? If you would like to understand, then read on.

Everlasting Peace

Paul knew contentment because he was at peace. We can live our lives with a punch when we have peace. I am not talking about peace in front of us. I am talking about peace inside us. The kind of peace that you have when you get a pink slip; you keep grinning. Your marriage seems to be on the rocks and you keep singing in the kitchen.. You feel like nobody cares, but you still have a song in your heart.

To start with the fundamental principle, it is imperative to know that you cannot create peace. Many spouses try to create peace and they create havoc and more headaches in the house and in their marriage. No one can create peace; only Christ can create peace. When Christ creates peace in your life, nothing will rock you and you will live life with a punch. When you have an inner peace, you can take on anything.

The Bible tells us that it was the "Father's good pleasure for all the fullness to dwell in Him" (Colossians 1:19. I love knowing that I am God's good pleasure --sinful and wretched--my righteousness was like filthy rags until I got to know Him. Even though He found me broken, busted, no good, doomed for hell, He says, "You are my good pleasure to redeem." I like that. The perfect, holy, righteous God, who sustains the universe, saw me leading a life without Him, and when I turned 12 years old, He sent a preacher so I could hear about Him. It was in my Father's design that I, in Guyana, South America, could sit in the back of the church with my buddies, hanging out, laughing and talking until somehow this preacher captured me with just two sentences that caused me to walk up the aisle and give my life to Jesus. It was His good pleasure.

"And through Him to reconcile all things to Himself, having made peace through the blood of His cross." (Colossians 1:20) He is saying, "When we as Gentiles had no hope. When we were doomed for hell, God sent His only Son Christ Jesus so that He would walk on earth, perfect without sin, die on the cross, bear our sin, cleanse us with His blood, so that God could forgive us." We are saved today not because of our good works. We are saved, because God found good pleasure in redeeming us through His Son.

Many of us are still searching for peace in our lives, because we are not at peace with God. You may be in church, you may have friends who are at peace with God, but unless you allow Him to cleanse you with His blood you will not experience peace with God. I consider this the most important portion of this book, because unless your faith leads you to accept Christ as your personal Savior, you will not be able to take steps to faith. If you have not, I urge you to invite Jesus in your heart as your Lord and King. Confess your sinfulness, repent of your sins, accept His sacrifice on your behalf, allow Him to cleanse you with His precious blood, and thank Him for the gift of eternal life.

When you are at peace with God, you don't have to worry about God being angry with you. Rather, you can always come to Him and tell Him everything. When you are at peace with God, you can pray boldly. You can call out to Him anywhere, anytime, anyhow, and talk to Him in Jesus' name. Once you talk to Him in Jesus' name, He says, "Because you are at peace with Me, I can hear you; I can respond to you; and I can work for you." You have punch in your life and can face each day with confidence knowing that you are the apple of His eye.

Recently, I saw a beautiful picture of a bird in the midst of a storm. It seems like the bird flew and landed on a rock, right next to the beach. Even though water is splashing everywhere, the bird continues to sit unperturbed on the rock! The author wrote, "Peace is when you depend on the Rock, and don't try to change His position." Most of us don't have peace in our lives, because we keep putting ourselves on the throne. Don't ever try to usurp God's position and act like the lord of your life. He is the Lord of the universe; enthrone him as the King of your life. The storms of life may be raging, but Jesus is the Rock; so depend on Him and let the peace of Christ rule in your heart.

The Bible says, "Deny yourself; pick up the cross and follow Christ" (Matthew 16:24). To do that, we need to get our petty attitudes out of the way. I always remind myself as a pastor, "Paul, keep the church focused on Christ so that you are out of the way. You could die tomorrow and the church will go on; because it is always about Christ and never about you."

We can enjoy peace in our lives when we walk in a manner worthy of our calling. The Bible expects us to live with "humility and gentleness, with patience, showing forbearance to one another in love, being diligent to preserve the unity of the Spirit in the bond of peace" (Ephesians 4:2). Let's dwell on this verse for a few moments. Never forget that God has called us in one body. Unity is crucial and is maintained by trusting God. Christ humbled Himself and came on earth. Am I right? When we choose to follow Christ, we manifest His humility. Gentleness is not being easy-going; it does not mean you cannot speak. Gentleness is being straightforward and not functioning with anger.

Patience is long-suffering. Patience says, "That person is wrong; I know they are wrong; they behaved wrong; they acted wrong. God, I am willing not to respond to them in anger." When you respond in anger, you automatically demonstrate patience. Christians have such intolerance for each other. We cannot tolerate each other. We act like we are better than the others and never make mistakes. If we can remember our frailty, we will be patient with other people.

God also wants us to forgive each other. Just as the Lord forgave you, so you should forgive. Forgiving is not forgetting. How can God forget? God does not forget. God remembers everything. Forgiving is saying, "Even though I remember what happened, I am still going to act in love towards you. I am going to treat you the way God tells me to treat you. I am going to interact with you the way God tells me to interact with you."

Again, learn to be thankful, and that will give you a punch in your life. The Bible does not suggest that you should be thankful; rather, the Bible makes it clear that it is the will of God for you to be thankful. Walk around saying, "Thank you, Lord," and watch how you get a punch in your life. Paul could be content in every state, because he had learned not to be anxious for anything.

I watched my son play football last night and they finally called him up to play after bouncing him around all season. He made one mistake and that's all he could think about. I said, "Son, you don't understand. They put you on the field. Did you look back on the sideline and see a long line of folks standing around while you were on the field? Son, you could have been standing right there. Thank the Lord and praise His name that you were on the field and not on the sideline.'" Life will be a punch when we learn not to be so fretful. Start saying: "Thank you, Lord!"

Wisdom from God

Every individual makes several decisions during a single day. Every time you decide to speak, you make a decision regarding the words you choose. Every time you decide to move, you make a decision regarding the path you take. How many of us wish that we had made better decisions with regard to our words, relationships,

Living Life with a Punch **157**

career choices, and financial expenditures? Wrong choices can definitely take the punch out of our lives. We need wisdom to make decisions, solve problems, and think through situations.

How can you and I achieve wisdom? Many people wait for some fire from heaven to come and hit them and make them wise instantly. Others believe that a person with gray hair is the person with wisdom. Wisdom comes from God, not age. A person could be gray-haired and rarely make the right decisions.

To attain wisdom, you have to pray for wisdom. James says, "But if any of you lacks wisdom, let him ask of God, who gives to all men generously and without reproach, and it will be given to him. But let him ask in faith without any doubting, for the one who doubts is like the surf of the sea driven and tossed by the wind." (James 1:5-6) When you come to God, don't come doubting and wondering if God is able to impart wisdom to you. Come to Him with faith, knowing that He would like to bless you with wisdom.

It is crucial to know that you cannot have wisdom without knowledge. When you refuse to study God's Word, yet pray for wisdom, you will not have the kind of wisdom that God has the potential to give you. You cannot gain knowledge by picking up the Bible on Sunday mornings and then forgetting about it the rest of the week. Knowledge is gained when you delve into the Word, and have a commitment to study it.

Reverend Spurgeon once visited a poor woman in a shabby senior home, where he saw a letter in a frame. Spurgeon asked the woman, "Have you ever read this letter?" She replied, "Oh, no, no. This letter is from a good friend. I took care of him a long time ago. He

Living Life with a Punch **158**

gave me this letter and I just appreciated his gesture so much that I framed it and put it on the wall, but I never read it."

Years ago this lady had faithfully taken care of an old man who was very sick. Sometimes the old man would remember to give her money, and sometimes he would forget. She would always show up, clean him and do all the necessary chores for the man--day after day, week after week, month after month, and year after year. His family left him alone and hardly came to see him, but this woman would show up and take care of him. And just before he died, the old man gave the woman this letter.

When Spurgeon read the letter, he told her to get ready to go out with him. They jumped in the pastor's car and they drove to the bank. When they showed the letter to the banker, the banker said, "The man had written to us and told us that he has a will and the person that comes with his letter is the one he wants to give his money to. His millions of dollars now belong to you." All these years this woman had been living in extremely poor conditions, while all the time she was a rich woman--all because she did not bother to read the letter.

Do you know that God wants you to live your life with a punch? Like the woman, we never take the time to read His will that He has written to us. Many of us have packed, stacked, and shelved His Book. God says, "If you ever read it, it is the Bread of Life. It is the only thing you need." "Man shall not live on bread alone, but on every word that proceeds out of the mouth of God" (Matthew 4:4). That means every word that comes from God. This is a Word that works and blesses. Why not pick it by faith, study it, and learn from it?

God says, "I want to transform your life by filling you with knowledge. I will renew your mind and help you to understand." Filling comes when we are willing to be accountable. If we are not willing to be accountable, we will never be filled with knowledge. I learned this lesson when my wife and I started raising our children. You could give children instructions many times, but if you don't say, "You need to make your bed or there will be consequences," they don't learn. Accountability helps you to gain deeper knowledge.

When we watch other people apply their knowledge; then we will learn from observation. Not surprisingly the Bible says, "Go make disciples, teaching them to observe all that I commanded you" (Matthew 28:19-20). That is why leadership in the church is supposed to be Christ-like. There has to be observation before there is a filling. Understand that wisdom is gained by praying, developing a knowledge base by studying the Word of God, and learning God's Word through accountability and observation.

Sometimes there are those decisions that require the specific guidance of the Holy Spirit. How does it work? When you decide to follow Him, God guides your path. Hebrews says, "When you practice the truth, I will train your senses to discern good and evil. (Hebrews 5:14) I will show you the right way. I will give you the confidence to move in the right direction. I will guide you—this person is for you, that job is not for you, this is not the financial decision you need to take." You are able to make those decisions when you are sensitive to the leading of the Holy Spirit. It is dangerous when we say, "I don't feel like it, so I am going to do this." Feelings emerge from our corrupt flesh, but you need to listen to the Holy Spirit if you want to live your life with a punch!

Living His Name

I used to travel for Tony Evans, Senior Pastor of Oak Cliff Bible Fellowship in Dallas, Texas. On one trip when I arrived in Norfolk, Virginia and got out of the plane, there was this guy waiting for me, and he said, "Dr. Cannings, let me take your bag." We were walking down the airport when the guy said, "Please go to the car, and I will bring your suitcase." I said, "Let's go there together." He got my suitcase and then I realized why he told me to go to the car. When I got to the car, a limousine--I mean a limousine was waiting for me. He said, "I have the newspaper for you and if you'd like to make some phone calls, please go ahead!" Do you know why I was given such a grand welcome? All of this was because of Tony Evans' name! I called the office and told Tony Evans, "When is your next trip? I want to go!"

When I was growing up, my dad had an account with Mr. Chan, the storeowner.

I would go to the store and say, "*Mr. Chan, my daddy needs this.*" "*You are the Cannings' boy?*"

"Yes, sir!"

"Alright. Come on in here." Mr. Chan would get the groceries and start sacking them.

I remember saying, "Mr. Chan?"

He replied, "What do you want, Paul."

I said, "I need a T-bun and chocolate milk."

He said, "Oh, no. I know your daddy, and your daddy did not ask for T-bun and chocolate milk."

One day I showed up at Mr. Chan's store and gave him the list. He worked through the list and when he had finished, he said, "Paul, look over at the corner of the counter."

It was my T-bun and chocolate milk. I said, "Thank you, Mr. Chan." He said, "No, thank your daddy."

During biblical times, names had a punch. If you mentioned somebody's name, "I am Abraham's son." "Okay, let me find you a wife." Bam, punch! If you said that you belonged to the Jewish race, you had punch because God did not let one soldier fall in war. God allowed them to walk through the Red Sea. God allowed them to go over the Jordan. God allowed them to walk around Jericho and the walls came crumbling down!

All the forces in heaven know Jesus' name and also the life, power, and glory that accompanies His name. His name is not just any name. His name is above all names. When you accept Christ as your Savior, you become the child of the King of kings and you can live your life with a punch, because of His name. This is an awesome truth. Never forget that you belong to the Almighty Lord who made you and shaped you in a special and unique way.

You don't have to run to others for abundant living. Your Daddy in heaven knows what you need and at the right time He will provide for you your T-bun and chocolate milk. Whatever you do, whether in word or indeed, you do all to the glory of God, because you do it in His name.

God says, "I Am who I Am. At the sound of My name, demons tremble." He is known as Yahweh, which means He keeps His covenant. No matter what you do, you will never lose your salvation. You may sin, but you can confess and turn to Him, and He will forgive your sins. No matter what storm, difficulty, or hardship you may face in your life, He is the Almighty God. His name gives me confidence and fills my heart with gladness.

He is Jehovah Jireh, the Lord who will provide. When I am sitting at my table, I have to say, "Thank you, Lord. I praise your name for giving me food to eat." He says, "I Am that I Am; I sustain myself. I don't need any help from anyone. I am Jehovah Nissi. I sealed you for the day of redemption. I am your banner." He is Shalom. He is your peace. He is El Shaddai. He is your source of blessings. He is Jehovah Shammah, the Lord is there; you are never alone.

There was a man who was coaching a football team. He noticed that the kids would go, hit each other and start crying. The coach brought all the football players to the side and he sat them down and he said, "Listen, what are you wearing?"

"We are wearing shoulder pads."

"What are you wearing?"

"A helmet."

What are you wearing?"

"Knee pads."

"What is this sport called?"

"Football."

"What do you do in football?"

"Tackle."

"Okay," he told one boy, "Go tackle him." Bam! Kid fell down and started to cry.

The coach walked to the crying kid, "Why are you crying, Son?"

"It hurts."

The coach said, "That's what happens in football. Do you still want to play?"

"Ummm-hmm."

He said, "All right, I want you to tackle the kid that tackled you."

Kid went out there and bam! The kid on the ground says, "That was nothing."

The coach said, "Why do you say that? Is it because it doesn't hurt?"

"No, Coach," the kid replied, "I am here to play football."

The coach said, "You just made the team!"

Christ is saying, "Put on your helmet of salvation. Put on the breastplate of righteousness. Take the sword of the Spirit, which is the Word of God. Once you put on the armor of God, go to war. Quit crying; quit talking about how bad it is; quit talking about how difficult it is. Instead, take the shield of faith with which you will be able to extinguish all the flaming missiles of the evil one" (Ephesians 6:10-17).

The Lord of lords has a wonderful plan for your life, so stand up and take your next step to faith today. It does not matter if you are at the bottom or even if you fell off during your earlier attempts. Praise God for the new day and determine not to live your life knocked out and knocked down. Put your confidence in Jesus and live your life with a punch.

May God bless you!

About Power Walk Ministries

Our Vision

The vision of Power Walk Ministries Inc. is to partner with churches to disciple leaders and others based on biblical training as modeled by Jesus Christ in an effort to impact the community and the world for the glory of God.

Our Mission

Power Walk Ministries' mission is to empower church leaders, families, singles and married couples through biblical training to positively change the home, church, and community for the glory of God. This is accomplished through leadership conferences, church consultations, radio ministries, video training, and the distribution of manuals and books locally, nationally, and internationally.

Our Focus

The focus of Power Walk Ministries is to `change lives one step at a time'. This empowers leaders from the inside out. When leaders are spiritually challenged, their walk with God becomes a powerful influence to others. This in turn affects not just churches, but also homes and communities. Spiritual growth along with training and material causes a leader to be productive for God's glory.

Dr. Paul Cannings' zeal for leaders of the local churches and parishioners is to equip and empower them to be effective in their respective ministries. As Dr. Cannings was led to start Power Walk ministries, he wanted to provide quality training with practical application so that leaders can both assess and address the pressing, spiritual needs of their local churches and communities.

As founder of a church, Dr. Cannings passionately desires to accomplish strength in the body of Christ bearing in mind the guidelines that were biblically developed. In his training tool, "Biblical Answers for the 21st Century Church," Dr. Cannings mentions, "I became involved in writing documents that served as a resource for many churches so that they can resolve issues from a "biblio-centric" perspective." His mandate is that in order to impact the world, it must begin with the leaders in the church. Equipping leaders with the appropriate tools to impact their church body is the heartbeat of Power Walk Ministries.

The Need

Power Walk Ministries exist to assist pastors, by providing material that guides them to stimulate spiritual growth in their leaders. Power Walk Ministries' goal is to meet the pressing needs of local churches, primarily in the urban communities, so that pastors and leaders can effectively minister to the diverse needs of leaders, parishioners and the community. It is designed to train these leaders to be great husbands, fathers, wives or mothers. This also teaches them how to work with their pastor as they seek to minister to the needs of congregants. It is designed to assist the pastor in establishing the Lord's vision in the life of the church and how to effectively expand the vision into the surrounding communities. Pastors and leaders are provided material and training so that they can quickly apply this information to the ongoing development of their churches, which in turn impacts the community to effectively bring about change.

How to Help

Becoming a Partner with Power Walk Ministries will truly be an awarding experience. Your contributions will help us reach and teach leaders in a variety of ways. Your contributions will help us to expand the distribution channels of our current book publications, expand conference dates and locations and to broaden radio and television production capabilities worldwide.

For more information or to donate, please contact:
Mayphous Collins
Power Walk Ministries
7350 TC Jester Blvd.
Houston, Texas 77088
281-260-7402
www.powerwalkministries.org

www.ingramcontent.com/pod-product-compliance
Lightning Source LLC
Chambersburg PA
CBHW032048150426
43194CB00006B/452